AMERICAN
WAR LIBRARY

✷ The American Revolution ✷

STRATEGIC BATTLES

Titles in the American War Library series include:

AMERICAN
WAR LIBRARY

The American Revolution

STRATEGIC BATTLES

by Nathan Aaseng

LUCENT
BOOKS®

THOMSON

GALE

San Diego • Detroit • New York • San Francisco • Cleveland • New Haven, Conn. • Waterville, Maine • London • Munich

Cover image: The Death of General Warren at the Battle
of Bunker Hill, June 17, 1775 by John Trumbull.

LIBRARY OF CONGRESS CATALOGING-IN-PUBLICATION DATA

Aaseng, Nathan.
    Strategic Battles / by Nathan Aaseng.
        p. cm. — (American War Library. American Revolution series)
Includes bibliographical references (p.) and index.
Summary: Reviews events leading up to the American Revolution and examines the
leaders, operations, and outcomes of major battles.
    ISBN 1-59018-221-9 (hardback : alk. paper)
    1. United States—History—Revolution, 1775-1783—Campaigns—Juvenile
literature. [1. United States—History—Revolution,1775-1783—Campaigns.]
I. Title. II. Series.
    E230 .A23 2003
    973.3'3—dc21
                                                              2002008588

Printed in the United States of America

★ Contents ★

A Nation Forged by War

The United States, like many nations, was forged and defined by war. Despite Benjamin Franklin's opinion that "There never was a good war or a bad peace," the United States owes its very existence to the War of Independence, one to which Franklin wholeheartedly subscribed. The country forged by war in 1776 was tempered and made stronger by the Civil War in the 1860s.

The Texas Revolution, the Mexican-American War, and the Spanish-American War expanded the country's borders and gave it overseas possessions. These wars made the United States a world power, but this status came with a price, as the nation became a key but reluctant player in both World War I and World War II.

Each successive war further defined the country's role on the world stage. Following World War II, U.S. foreign policy redefined itself to focus on the role of defender, not only of the freedom of its own citizens, but also of the freedom of people everywhere. During the cold war that followed World War II until the collapse of the Soviet Union, defending the world meant fighting communism. This goal, manifested in the Korean and Vietnam conflicts, proved elusive, and soured the American public on its achievability. As the United States emerged as the world's sole superpower, American foreign policy has been guided less by national interest and more by protecting international human rights. But as involvement in Somalia and Kosovo proves, this goal has been equally elusive.

As a result, the country's view of itself changed. Bolstered by victories in World Wars I and II, Americans first relished the role of protector. But, as war followed war in a seemingly endless procession, Americans began to doubt their leaders, their motives, and themselves. The Vietnam War especially caused people to question the validity of sending its young people to die in places where they were not particularly wanted and for people who did not seem especially grateful.

While the most obvious changes brought about by America's wars have been geopolitical in nature, many other aspects of society have been touched. War often does not bring about change directly, but acts instead like the catalyst in a chemical reaction, accelerating changes already in progress.

Some of these changes have been societal. The role of women in the United States had been slowly changing, but World War II put thousands into the workforce and into uniform. They might have gone back to being housewives after the war, but equality, once experienced, would not be forgotten.

Likewise, wars have accelerated technological change. The necessity for faster airplanes and more destructive bombs led to the development of jet planes and nuclear energy. Artificial fibers developed for parachutes in the 1940s were used in clothing of the 1950s.

Lucent Books' American War Library covers key wars in the development of the nation. Each war is covered in several volumes, to allow for more detail and context, and to provide volumes on often neglected subjects, such as the kamikazes of World War II, or the weapons used in the Civil War. As with all Lucent books, notes, annotated bibliographies, and appendixes such as glossaries give students a launching point for further research. In addition, sidebars and archival photographs enhance the text. Together, each volume in the American War Library will aid students in understanding how America's wars have shaped and changed its politics, economics, and society.

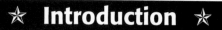
Former Friends– Different Strategies

From 1756 to 1763, American colonists stood side by side with troops from Great Britain on the battlefield as they fought the French for dominance in eastern North America. Eventually the British and their colonial allies prevailed, but scarcely had the ink dried on the treaty sealing their victory in this Seven Years' War (also called the French and Indian War) than a rift began growing between the victors. Barely a decade later, this dispute would escalate until the former friends turned their guns on each other in the American Revolution.

Resentment over Tax Policy

The gulf between England and its American colonies had many causes, but was most obviously rooted in a difference of opinion on the financing of military defense. The British government argued that the Americans were not paying their fair share for defending the colonies from the French and Indian enemies. As one remedy for this, the British government passed the Revenue Act of 1764, or Sugar Act, which imposed a tax on certain goods and restricted American trade with countries other than Britain. The Americans resented such interference with their commerce. "One single Act of Parliament has set people a-thinking, in six months, more than they had done in their whole lives before,"[1] fumed influential lawyer James Otis of Boston. A year later, the British Parliament fanned the flames of resentment by passing the Stamp Act, which levied a tax on such things as legal documents, newspapers, calendars, and even playing cards. What most infuriated the colonists about this policy of taxation was that they had no representation in Parliament, which was passing these laws. In that regard, they believed they were being denied rights belonging to all British citizens.

American Defiance Grows Bolder

At this point, few Americans were thinking of anything beyond getting policy changed.

British troops fire into a crowd of American colonists in an incident that became known as the Boston Massacre.

When some advocated open resistance to the government, Benjamin Franklin responded

a firm loyalty to the Crown and faithful adherence to the government of this nation, which it is the safety as well as honour of the colonies to be connected with, will always be the wisest course for you and I to take, whatever may be the madness of the populace or their blind leaders, who can only bring themselves and country into trouble and draw on greater burthens [burdens] by acts of rebellious tendency.[2]

In fact, Parliament did respond to American protests by repealing the Stamp Act in 1766. But it kept looking for alternatives and in 1767 passed the Townshend Acts, which imposed new import taxes on the colonies. This met with renewed outrage that occasionally spilled over into violence against British officials charged with collecting the taxes. Further resentment over a law requiring the colonists to house and finance British troops whose job was to enforce these unpopular laws led to a confrontation in Boston on March 5, 1770. When an angry mob confronted British soldiers, the troops eventually fired on the crowd, killing five in an incident the colonists named the Boston Massacre.

Again, the British government backed down, repealing all the provisions of the Townshend Acts except for the tax on tea. This tax was retained, said England's Lord North, because "the authority of the mother country, if it is now unsupported, will be relinquished forever: a total repeal cannot be thought of till America is prostrate at our feet." [3]

It was tea that sparked the next crisis in 1773, when the British administration tried to rescue the floundering East India Company by giving it a monopoly on the tea trade in America. Although the

Lexington: First Shots of the War

Some history books refer to a "Battle of Lexington," but what took place there can hardly be considered a battle. As the British marched toward Concord at the first hint of dawn, on April 19, 1775, they came across a disorganized band of about seventy militiamen in the small town of Lexington. Originally, twice that number had assembled upon hearing news of the British advance, but many had grown tired of waiting for the British and left.

The militia were led by former Indian fighter John Parker, who earlier had told his men to stand their ground but not fire unless fired upon. But at the sight of hundreds of British regulars advancing on them, Parker realized that his men would not stand a chance against them, and he began to pass the word that they should disperse. The two sides disputed what happened next, with each accusing the other of firing first. William Cumming and Hugh Rankin, in *The Fate of a Nation*, reported events as remembered by American militiaman Sylvanus Wood:

The officer (British major John Pitcairn) then swung his sword and said, "Lay down your arms, you damned rebels, or you are all dead men!—Fire!" Some guns were fired by the British at us from the first platoon, but no person was killed or hurt, being charged only with powder. Just at this time Captain Parker ordered every man to take care of himself. The company immediately dispersed; and while the company was dispersing and leaping over the wall, the second platoon of the British fired, and killed some of our men. There was not a gun fired by any of Captain Parker's, within my knowledge.

Light wounds suffered by one British soldier indicates that some on the American side did fire. But regardless of who actually fired the first shot, it was the British who unleashed a deadly volley while Pitcairn frantically called on his men to stop. When the smoke cleared, eight militiamen lay dead and ten were wounded.

colonists actually benefited from the deal by getting tea at a cheaper price than before, American merchants objected to the government again taking control of commerce. On December 16, 1773, a band of radicals boarded British vessels in Boston Harbor and dumped the tea overboard.

Great Britain Cracks Down

Incensed by this vandalism, Parliament responded by passing laws that the Americans termed the "Intolerable Acts." Included among the provisions was the closing of Boston Harbor and restrictions on local self-government. General Thomas Gage arrived in Boston on May 17, 1774, to take charge of the enforcement of these laws.

In general, British officers believed the Americans would submit so long as the government stood up to the rabble-rousers. "As to what you hear of their taking up arms to resist the force of England, it is merely bullying, and will go no further than words," wrote one officer. "Whenever it comes to blows, he that can run fastest will think himself best off."[4]

General Gage agreed that strong action was needed to keep the colonies in line. Upon the urging of his government, he made plans in the spring of 1775 to crack down on the rebellion. On the night of April 18, his troops began a surprise march to the town of Concord, sixteen miles to the west, to seize a large supply of guns and ammunition that the rebels were reported to have cached there. Alert Boston citizens, however, discovered the departure and soon knew exactly what Gage was up to. Messengers such as Boston silversmith Paul Revere rode furiously through the countryside to warn residents of the British march.

The War Begins

When the British soldiers approached the village of Lexington at dawn on April 19, neither the colonists nor the British government had any enthusiasm for war. Armies were difficult to recruit and train, and expensive to maintain. Most colonists, meanwhile, still retained some loyalty to England. Even those who did not had to realize that England boasted the best-trained and best-equipped soldiers in the world. Few had any hope of defeating them in battle.

At Lexington, however, a small company of colonists made a brief stand. They were quickly dispersed by gunfire from the British, leaving eight rebels dead and ten wounded. While the affair was so brief that it could hardly be called a battle, it marked the point of no return in relations between the colonists and the British.

The British then marched on to Concord, but by the time they arrived, the weapons and ammunition had been moved. At the North Bridge, the British found their way blocked by a much larger group of Americans than had faced them at Lexington. In the exchange of fire, several on both sides fell. The British retreated, and by noon they began marching back to Boston. By this time, word of the

American colonists confront British soldiers at Concord's North Bridge.

killings at Lexington had swept through the countryside, and Americans swarmed to exact their revenge. The British came under constant sniper fire from houses and from behind trees, rocks, and fences. After running into two larger ambushes, their ranks grew dangerously thin. At about two in the afternoon, however, a relief party of one thousand men arrived from Boston. Its commander, Lord Hugh Percy, made clear the state of the retreating British when he commented, "I had the happiness of saving them from inevitable destruction."[5] In the march from Concord, 273 British soldiers were killed, while the Americans lost 95.

Without either side having planned or desired it, war was upon them. News of the Concord fighting reached Philadelphia in May; by June the Continental Congress had authorized the formation of a national army and had named George Washington to command it. The American government continued to search for a negotiated settlement over the next few months. But once the independent spirit had been roused, there was no turning back. For the next eight years, the colonists and the British would be in a state of war.

War Strategies

The Americans and British had opposite aims in their military strategy for the war. After the opening skirmishes in the conflict, the aim of the American army became basically survival. Its leaders knew that they were no match for the British in a head-to-head confrontation. The British were complete masters of the sea, and their troops were well-trained, professional soldiers, while most of the colonists were amateurs. Also, British factories

The Continental Congress named George Washington to command the national army. Below, Washington assumes command at Cambridge in 1775.

could churn out far more military supplies than the Americans. The Americans had a loosely organized government that understood little about supplying troops, even if it had the money to buy the supplies, which it seldom did. Conditions in the American Continental army were often so wretched that officers faced a constant struggle to recruit and retain enough soldiers to stay in the field.

As a result, the Americans generally played not to lose. They avoided major battles with the main force of the British wherever possible. The only exceptions were the occasions when the need to maintain public morale demanded that they make a stand—in defending the key cities of New York and Philadelphia, for example. In addition, the rebels constantly sought to isolate British army units so they could win without having to engage the bulk of the British army.

The British, in contrast, were under the clock. The government was well aware that it could not afford a long and costly war, either politically or economically. Their strategy consisted of trying to lure the Americans into major actions

where they could destroy the American armies and break the spirit of the rebels. Britain's strategy took the form of three major campaigns: a grand scheme to cut off New England from the other colonies; a

Trying to Stop a War

Even after the open conflict at Lexington and Concord, most Americans initially opposed independence from Great Britain, much less fighting a war over it. When the Second Continental Congress met on May 10, 1775, it authorized the formation of a national army but only as a precaution. Congress continued to present American grievances to the British government in hopes of getting it to change policy and thus prevent further strife. As late as December 1775, long after the Battle of Bunker Hill and the American capture of Fort Ticonderoga, the Congress declared its continuing allegiance to the king of England.

In the fall of 1775, however, Lord George Germain had taken over as the British secretary of state for the colonies. He agreed with King George III that the government must deal firmly and uncompromisingly with the rebels, whose actions he considered treason. The British struck back harshly, burning the city of Falmouth, Maine, in October 1775, and implementing a law that stopped all trade with the American colonies two months later. In addition, rumors began to surface of British encouragement of Indian and slave uprisings, use of prostitutes to spread smallpox infection, and recruitment of German professional soldiers to fight against the Americans.

In this climate of fear and uncertainty, the words of Thomas Paine touched off a wildfire of revolutionary fervor. Broke and disowned as a disgrace by his own mother, Paine had taken up journalism at the age of thirty-seven and at the same time was converted to the Patriot cause. His *Common Sense* pamphlet, published in January 1776, attacked the British monarchy and eloquently urged Americans to fight for their independence. Paine's words struck a nerve in American hearts. By the end of the year, 120,000 copies were printed, making it, in proportion to the population, the best-selling work in U.S. history.

Growing anger at Britain's harsh crackdown combined with the eloquence of writers like Paine persuaded American leaders that they had no choice but to make a clean break with England. On June 7, Richard H. Lee of Virginia moved that the Congress declare the "United Colonies" independent from Great Britain. The motion passed, and a committee was appointed to craft the words of such a declaration. This Declaration of Independence, authored primarily by Thomas Jefferson of Virginia, made its way to the Congress in July. With Jefferson fuming on the sidelines, Congress made nearly one hundred revisions to Jefferson's masterpiece and passed the measure on July 4, 1776. With that open declaration of what the British government considered treason, all hopes for a peaceful resolution to the conflict ended.

campaign to seize key American cities and destroy Washington's Continental army in the mid-Atlantic colonies; and finally a drive through the South to crush resistance and bolster those colonists who were loyal to the British government.

Throughout most of the war, the British held the upper hand. But like the proverbial cat with nine lives, the American army survived one near-death experience after another to repeatedly deny the British the decisive victory they were seeking.

Chapter 1

Bunker Hill

Following the disaster of the march to Concord, the British troops in Boston found themselves in an unexpectedly perilous position. An American force of more than 15,000 controlled the two narrow necks of land that connected Boston with the mainland, meaning that the 6,500-man British garrison could not move, much less impose order on the rebellious New England colonies.

The British government signaled its displeasure with the performance of General Gage and indicated the seriousness with which they viewed the American challenge by sending three highly regarded major generals to Boston. The three, William Howe, Henry Clinton, and John Burgoyne, arrived by ship on May 25, 1775, along with reinforcements that brought the British garrison to ten thousand.

Looking for a Breakout Point

Burgoyne reflected the British government's disgust at seeing one of the finest armies in the world bottled up by what they considered to be a rabble of farmers. "What! Ten thousand King's troops shut up?" Burgoyne reportedly said upon landing. "Well, let us get in, and we'll soon find elbow room."[6] As the generals looked for a way to break out of their defensive position, their first order of business was to eliminate the threat to their safety by securing the high ground overlooking Boston—Dorchester Heights to the south and Bunker Hill on the Charlestown Peninsula to the north. If the Americans were to obtain artillery pieces and place them on those hills, they could lob shells into the trapped British army at will. The generals made plans to occupy Dorchester Heights, then advance upon rebel positions from the south and west. However, thanks to an efficient spy network in Boston and General Burgoyne's apparent carelessness in openly discussing his intentions, the Americans learned of the plan almost immediately. On the night of June 16, two days before the British were to make their move, a group of one thousand Massachusetts militia and two hundred volunteers from Connecticut crossed the narrow spit of land from the west and began occupying the Charlestown Peninsula.

Their actions forced the British to take a new tack by sending troops to fortify Bunker Hill. As Burgoyne described the situation, "On the 17th, at dawn of day, we found the enemy had pushed entrenchments with great diligence during the night, on the Heights of Charlestown, and we evidently saw that every hour gave them fresh strength; it therefore became necessary to alter our plan, and attack on that side."[7]

Loose Collection of Volunteers

According to historian George Bancroft, the rebels' decision to defend the peninsula "was so sudden that no fit preparations could be made."[8] The colonial soldiers who rushed to confront the disciplined, highly trained and heavily armed British force had precious little ammunition and no effective artillery. The army that assembled on the peninsula was a loose collection of volunteers of varying abilities, experience, and weapons. Furthermore, there was little structure to the colonial military. Operations around Boston were loosely supervised by the American Committee, under the leadership of General Artemas Ward. But the chain of command in

The Amateur Army

Throughout the war, the Americans relied heavily on militia to do the fighting rather than training a large national army. Militia were part-time, amateur soldiers, described by Mark Mayo Boatner III, in *Encyclopedia of the American Revolution,* as "Ill-trained farmers, citizens, shopkeepers, ready to leave their work and fight when the enemy approached." Their short-term enlistments made a shambles of any long-range planning; they were known to leave the army and head for home the second their term of commitment was up, even if it was on the eve of a major battle. Because they were subject only to state authorities, it was extremely difficult for American generals to exercise any control over them. There were many instances of militia refusing to fight for one leader or another whom they viewed as lacking either the authority or the skill to direct them. Furthermore, the militia's lack of training made them unreliable at best in the face of enemy fire; many threw down their

weapons and ran as soon as the lines of British troops drew near.

Many American leaders, such as George Washington, argued strongly against this reliance on militia, and their attempts to recruit, train, and supply a large national army yielded poor results. Washington, in a letter that appears in John Rhodehamel's *The American Revolution: Writings from the War of Independence,* early in the war observed, "The unhappy policy of short inlistments, and a dependence upon Militia will, I fear, prove the downfall of our cause."

On the other hand, militia acquitted themselves well in many key battles such as Bunker Hill, Bennington, Kings Mountain, and Cowpens. Military historians note that the militia fought with passion when aroused and performed admirably so long as they were led by experienced leaders who understood the limitations of this untrained, unpredictable fighting force.

the field was seldom clear. Making decisions in the field often involved arguments, persuasion, and compromise.

Fortunately for the Americans, Colonel William Prescott was one of the leaders assigned to take command of the peninsula operations. The forty-nine-year-old Prescott had performed so admirably almost thirty years earlier in fighting for the British army that the Royal Army had offered him a command, an honor seldom bestowed upon colonists. Prescott, however, had declined and had enjoyed a peaceful life as a gentleman farmer until drawn into the Revolution.

Prescott had orders to organize his defensive lines at Bunker Hill, the highest point on the peninsula. Nestled between the mouths of the Charles River and the Mystic River, the peninsula was only a mile in length and little more than a mile wide. But in surveying the land, he saw the advantages of meeting the British landing forces closer to the landing beaches, on Breed's Hill. After considerable debate with other militia leaders who insisted that their orders specifically said to fortify Bunker Hill, the colonists agreed to a compromise—Breed's pasture between the two locations. Under the direction of engineer Richard Grudley, they began to construct defensive works.

British Assault Plan

The British officers studied the Americans' activities through a spyglass. Upon learning that Prescott was commanding the colonists, General Gage asked an aide, "Will he fight?" The answer was: "Yes, Sir, depend on it, to

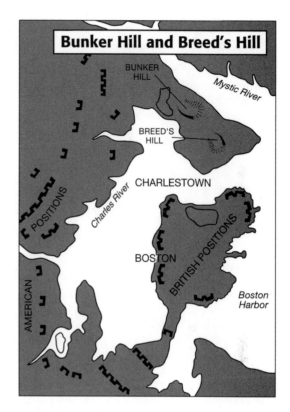

the last drop of blood in him, but I cannot answer for his men."[9]

In their war counsel, General Clinton proposed landing a force on the Charlestown neck to the rear of the American troops and thus trapping them on the peninsula. The other generals, however, argued that it would be a needless risk to place a force between the Americans on the peninsula and the larger American army that was located inland. In the end, they agreed on Howe's plan to land on the eastern shore. They would then attack the American left with just enough strength to keep them occupied while another force advanced along the Mystic River and flanked the Americans from the north.

The Red Coats

The British army has been ridiculed through the ages for their style of fighting in the American Revolution. They almost seemed to be inviting defeat as they showed up for battles wearing bright red coats that made them clear targets for the enemy and marching in straight rows directly into enemy fire.

In fact, however, the strategy was not as mindless as it appears on the surface. The standard weapon at the time was the musket, which was inefficient and inaccurate even in the most skilled hands. The loading, priming, and firing of a musket required eight separate steps. Few soldiers could manage to fire as many as three rounds in a minute. A musket could be fired with dependable accuracy only at a distance of eighty yards or less. If the battle took place in rain, they were not likely to fire at all.

When advancing upon a massed enemy, the British generally marched in columns rather than lines. This presented few targets at any one time to the enemy. As a result, the enemy could not begin firing upon them until the British advanced to within eighty yards, if they could fire at all. The enemy could not get many of them in a concentrated volley. In most cases, the British could exchange fire with the enemy and then be upon them with minimum loss before they could reload and fire. Because of this fact, the British tended to rely more on bayonets than muskets in battle. Frequently, as at Bunker Hill,

they did not even bother loading their weapons, as they could deal more quickly and effectively with their bayonets.

Even the red coats served a useful purpose of intimidation, especially when dealing with inexperienced troops. The British counted on the splendor of their uniforms, crisp lines, and unshakable discipline in the face of fire to put fear into the enemy. Frequently, it worked. The spectacle of a British attack often scared militia so badly that they fled without firing a shot.

At Bunker Hill, the colonists admitted to being frightened by the majesty of the British charge. According to one rebel quoted in *The American Story: The Revolutionaries,* by Russell B. Adams, "They looked too handsome to fire upon but we had to do it." This British tradition of attack, however, ran into problems when fighting Americans who had no interest in or respect for tradition. British officers were easy to spot and often stood exposed to fire. When fighting foes with similar codes of honor in war, this was no problem because it was considered barbaric to target officers. Americans had no qualms about this, and as a result the British often lost much of their leadership during a battle. Furthermore, in wilderness areas, where taking advantage of cover was a key aspect of fighting, the British method was totally impractical and contributed to their problems in the Saratoga campaign.

In the morning of June 17, the Americans continued their feverish efforts to dig trenches and construct fortifications while the British began firing at them from warships. One direct hit obliterated a rebel soldier, Asa Pollard, as he brought water down for the workers from Bunker Hill. This so unnerved the Americans that they ceased

their work. Colonel Prescott quickly had the man buried and then climbed up onto the wall they were building and paced in full view of the British. "It was a one-in-a-million shot," he scoffed. "See how close they come to hitting me!" [10] Prescott's courage inspired the jittery Americans to resume their labors.

Delayed Start and American Adjustments

The British had hoped for an early start for their attack, but they had to wait for the tide to come in before they launched the barges carrying their soldiers. As a result, it was early afternoon before Howe, who commanded the attack force, came ashore at Moulton's Point with his 1,550 soldiers. Spectators crowded on every rooftop, hill, and boat mast in Boston Harbor to watch the battle. They so outnumbered the actual participants that the scene resembled an outdoor theater. The Americans offered no resistance to the landing but waited in their defensive positions. Noting the position of the British troops, Prescott guessed that the main attack would be on his left. He positioned two hundred men under Thomas Knowlton behind a rail fence slightly to the left and rear of his lines.

Seeing how well the Americans had strengthened their positions in the past hours, Howe realized that he would need more men for the assault. He sent for the seven hundred men in his reserve units to join him on the peninsula. But this delay allowed time for the arrival of General John Stark and his two hundred New Hampshire riflemen on the scene. Stark noticed that while Knowlton had strengthened the American left, he had left the beach on that side of the peninsula open to attack. He had his men haul stones up from the riverbank to form a barricade on the beach right where Howe intended his fiercest attack.

Seeing this, Howe decided to make use of the British warships to clear the way. He asked his admiral to send a ship up the Mystic River and drive off the exposed Americans with cannon shot. To his frustration, the admiral declined. He had no charts of the river and did not want to risk grounding a ship. Adding to Howe's problems, those in charge of artillery supplies

Colonists perch atop buildings in Boston for a view of the battle occurring on Bunker Hill.

had made a crucial error. The cannons that the British had brought were designed to fire six-pound balls but had been supplied with twelve-pound balls instead.

A Surprising Stand

Despite these problems, the British began their attack in the heat of the afternoon with an air of contempt for the rabble in front of them. In the words of author Robert Middlekauff

The old casual feeling of superiority that puffed up imperial heads when they dealt with the 'provincials' may

have clouded [Howe's] judgment as he sent his troops straight into the prepared defense. [11]

In the main attack along the beach on the American left, the British marched forward four abreast. They expected to weather the initial round of fire from the enemy and then fall upon them with deadly bayonets. As a result, they did not bother to load their muskets. Stark, however, positioned his men three deep. When the British drew close, the first line opened up a withering fire. Many British soldiers fell, but the rest advanced to deal with the

Dr. Joseph Warren: General in the Front Ranks

The greatest loss for the Patriots at Bunker Hill was the death of Dr. Joseph Warren. Born in Roxbury, Massachusetts, in 1741, Warren was a brilliant student who graduated from Harvard University at the age of eighteen. He then opened a thriving medical practice in Boston, where he became involved in St. Andrews Lodge, a social group that included some of Boston's most radical political figures.

Warren joined their cause. His courage, integrity, and leadership skills quickly made him one of the most respected men on the continent. He achieved considerable fame for delivering an impassioned address on the anniversary of the Boston Massacre in front of British officers who had been sent to quell the city's unrest. The British barred the door of the building, planning to arrest him, but he climbed through a back window and got away. In the early 1770s, he served as Grand Master of Masons for the entire continent of North America and was named president pro tem of the Massachusetts Provincial Congress.

It was Warren who learned of the British plans to march on Concord in April 1774, and he sent Paul

Revere and others on their ride into the countryside to warn the Patriots. So highly regarded was Warren among colonists that on June 14, the Provincial Congress commissioned him a major general in the army even though he had no experience or training. Recognizing his limitation, however, Warren refused to take command. Over the strenuous objections of his fellow generals, he insisted on carrying a musket and serving as a private on the front line of the battlefield.

Warren apparently had a premonition of what was to happen to him on Bunker Hill. The night before the battle, according to Robert W. Williams III, in his brief sketch of Warren appearing on the website www.warrentavern.com, he asked one of his daughters to "drink a glass of wine with me for the last time, for I shall go to the hill tomorrow and never come off." Fearless to the end, Warren stayed at his post in the front line until it was too late to retreat. He died of a musket shot to the head, and the British threw his body into a ditch with the rest of the American dead. It was later found, and Warren was reburied with honors.

rebels. To their shock, the first line of Americans withdrew, and a second line laid down another deadly volley. Before the reeling British could recover, the third line opened up.

Unable to advance into such a fearsome barrage and with no loaded weapons of their own with which to return fire, the British forward lines were annihilated. They had no choice but to retreat, leaving ninety-six of their number dead on the beach.

On the other side of the peninsula, the British made good on a threat to burn the town of Charlestown. After their troops reported drawing fire from snipers in houses in that area, British warships set the town ablaze by firing red-hot cannon balls into the buildings.

Don't Fire Until You See the Whites of Their Eyes

Howe was forced to alter his strategy. He shifted his assault on the American left from the beach to Knowlton's rail fence, while the main force attacked the American positions on Breed's pasture. The British were hindered on this attack by marching with a full load of from 50 to 125 pounds of gear per man—supplies for an extended engagement. Their disciplined lines broke apart as soldiers struggled over the irregular ground, through the tall grass, and got hung up on fences.

The Americans, aware of their shortage of ammunition, dared not waste a shot. This led to the famous command, often at-

American officer Israel Putnam urged his men to fire at the "handsome coats" of British commanders.

tributed to Prescott, to not fire until the attackers "were near enough for us to see the whites of their eyes." Another American officer, Israel Putnam of Connecticut, was more specific. "Fire low," he told his men. "Take aim at the waistbands—pick off the commanders—aim at the handsome coats."[12]

As at the beach, the Americans, sheltered behind their six-foot-high earthworks, cut loose with one devastating volley after another from close range. With a heroic display of discipline, the British kept reforming their lines and attempting to advance, with horrific results. In some companies, nine out of ten soldiers fell dead or wounded, and again the British were forced to retreat. One British officer fumed that it was "downright butchery to lead the men afresh against those lines."[13]

Ammunition Shortage

Howe was stunned to see that instead of the expected easy victory, his forces were reeling on the brink of a humiliating defeat. Aware that the survival of his army was at stake, he had no choice but to send the last of his reserves and try a third and final assault on the hill. This attack might have fared no better than the others but for the fact that the Americans had used nearly all their available ammunition in fighting off the second attack. Neither reinforcements nor supplies had come from the American forces on the mainland. The defenders, many of whom had worked all night constructing defensive works and had gone all day with virtually nothing to drink, were dehydrated and exhausted. They now faced heavy fire from British cannons, which had been refitted with proper ammunition.

To conserve ammunition, the Americans had to wait until the British were within forty yards of their positions before firing. That meant that this time the British needed to absorb only the initial brutal volley and part of another before they reached the Americans' forward positions. Once they closed in on the defenders, it was the Americans who were in mortal danger. In close, hand-to-hand fighting, their muskets and rifles were useless, and few of them had bayonets with which to defend themselves. The British, well-trained in the art of bayonet warfare, began to pour over the defenses. Thirsting for revenge on the men who had slaughtered their companions, British troops used their bayonets to murderous advantage. Showing courage that astonished the British officers, the Americans stayed in the lines, firing what ammunition they had left, until the last possible moment. Some stayed too long; thirty of Prescott's men were trapped in a redoubt —a defensive enclosure—and killed. The slaughter would have been worse had it not been for the steady fire of Stark's men covering the retreat of the main body of Americans as they fell back from their position near the river.

The confused, exhausted, and scared American troops were in no condition to make a serious stand higher up at Bunker Hill. Fortunately for them, the British were also spent from their day's efforts. They stopped to regroup after taking Breed's Hill. By the time they received the order to advance, the Americans had escaped across the neck of the Charlestown Peninsula.

In many ways, the Americans had been extremely fortunate in the conflict. Had Howe attacked immediately upon landing, he probably would have overrun the American left along the Mystic River before Stark had a chance to deploy there. Most importantly, as historian W. J. Wood points out, "At Bunker Hill the rawest of American militia were led in the right places by veteran officers who knew how to handle militia from their experience in the French and Indian War."[14] Prescott and Stark, two of the ablest commanders in the colonies, happened to be exactly where they were needed during the battle.

Painful Victory and Lessons Learned

It was generally accepted at the time that the army that held the field following a bat-tle was the victor, and that meant that the British were victorious at Bunker Hill. According to Wood, "Prevailing public feeling was that the battle was not only a defeat but a military misadventure that never should have been attempted."[15] Many Americans leveled bitter criticism at the American general, Artemas Ward, for not giving his troops more support.

British soldiers close in on the American lines during the Battle of Bunker Hill.

But the public perception soon changed. British losses on the day had been 226 dead and 828 wounded, compared to American casualties of 140 dead and 271 wounded. British general Henry Clinton described the battle as "a dear-bought victory. Another such would have ruined us."[16] In the end, the British not only suffered a devastating loss of troops but were unable to break out of Boston and establish a secure position. In March 1776, after the Americans obtained cannons and began lobbing shells at them from Dorchester Heights, the British finally evacuated the city by ship.

Perhaps the most significant result of the battle was the confidence it leant to the Americans. They had stunned not only the British but also themselves with their ability to stand up to and inflict punishment on what was regarded as the best army in the world. In the first major battle of the Revolutionary War, commonly called the Battle of Bunker Hill despite its location at Breed's Hill, the British lost their reputation as an invincible fighting force. For the first time, many Americans came to believe that their revolution could actually succeed. Upon hearing reports of the battle, American statesman Benjamin Franklin recognized the significance of the event, exclaiming, "The King has lost his colonies."[17]

This newfound confidence proved to be a curse as well as a blessing. The outstanding performance of the American militia at Bunker Hill convinced many Americans that they could defeat the British without a formal, organized military. As a result, when George Washington, who had been named overall commander of the colonial military forces two days before the Battle of Bunker Hill, requested that the Continental Congress make provision for a trained army of forty thousand with a long-term commitment, the Congress ignored him. Washington was authorized an army of twenty thousand with a one-year commitment and had trouble attracting even close to that number. While the British learned from their mistakes at Bunker Hill and made adjustments, the main colonial war effort against the British in New York would flounder largely because of the shaky performance of raw, undisciplined troops against seasoned British regulars.

Chapter 2

Quebec

Not every battle of the American Revolution was fought on the home soil of the rebelling colonists. In the heady days that followed the surprisingly effective performance of the colonials at Bunker Hill, the Americans made the bold decision to expand the war into Canada.

Canada "Must Be Ours"

This undertaking involved much more than a rash outburst of overconfidence and a desire to take the fight to the British. It stemmed, at least in part, from American fears of Canadian expansionism. Although both the American and Canadian colonists were subject to British rule, they were not the friendliest of neighbors. The social and political barriers that had long existed due to Canada's historical connection to France remained. American suspicions of its northern neighbor had been smoldering ever since 1763, when the British government recognized Canada's boundaries as extending southward to the Ohio River. Americans believed that this land, which included the present-day states of Ohio and Michigan, should be theirs and resented the limitation this placed on American expansion. This extension of Canadian territory, along with British attempts to maintain peace between colonists and Indians by prohibiting expansion of settlements west of the Appalachian Mountains, infuriated Americans eager to claim new lands.

In 1775, the American Continental Congress approached the Canadians in hopes of finding a peaceful solution to the boundary issue and to recruit the Canadians to the cause of fighting for freedom from England. Canada, however, declined to take part in the fight.

On May 10, 1775, an American force led by Ethan Allen and Benedict Arnold surprised and captured the strategic but poorly maintained British Fort Ticonderoga along the New York–Vermont border. The fall of this military stronghold left the major Canadian cities of Montreal and

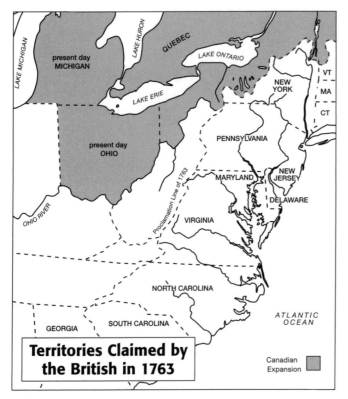

Territories Claimed by the British in 1763

Canadian Expansion

Quebec vulnerable to invasion from the south. A number of influential Americans argued in favor of taking this opportunity. By invading and occupying Canada, the Americans could not only settle any boundary disputes in their favor, but also reduce the chances that the British could mount an invasion of America using Canada as a base. As Robert Morris of Pennsylvania argued, "[Canada] must be ours . . . shou'd it fall into the hands of the Enemy, they will soon raise a Nest of Hornets at our backs that will sting us to the quick."[18] The "Hornets" to which Morris referred were warriors from the powerful Iroquois tribes of the northwest forests. Morris was among many Amer-

icans who feared that the British would stir up these Indians to fight against the American settlers on the frontier.

Although Canada was ruled by the British at that time, most of the inhabitants of Montreal and Quebec were French, the traditional enemies of the British. Given this fact, the Americans anticipated that an invading force would draw considerable aid from Canadian civilians. Therefore, on June 27, 1775, the Continental Congress authorized American forces to invade Canada.

Two-Pronged Attack

With the approval and advice of newly commissioned commander in chief George Washington, a two-pronged attack was set in motion. One army, led by General Philip Schuyler, commander of the Northern Department of the colonial military, was to advance up the Hudson River–Lake Champlain waterway in New York and capture Montreal. A second, under Benedict Arnold, would cut through the Maine wilderness to the east and capture Quebec City.

On August 27, Schuyler's army of seventeen hundred untrained Connecticut and New York militia crossed the Canadian border and set up a base of operations at Ile aux Noix. The expedition started poorly. Two attempts to capture the key British-held Fort St. John's were so badly bungled that the

Americans scattered in disarray before they even got near the fort. The army was then greatly weakened by an epidemic. Among the victims was General Schuyler who, on September 16, turned over command to General Richard Montgomery and returned south to recuperate.

On September 25, Ethan Allen, who had made a name for himself during the capture of Fort Ticonderoga, worked out a plan with Colonel John Brown for capturing Montreal: Brown would strike from the north while Allen attacked the city from the south. The British commander at Montreal, Sir Guy Carleton, learned of the plan, however. He sent a strong force to ambush Allen's army before it could attack, while it was isolated. Surrounded, Allen was forced to surrender his entire command, and he himself was sent to England on a prison ship.

Meanwhile, on September 13, Arnold embarked with 1,050 volunteers on an expedition up the Kennebec River in Maine, a route suggested by Washington. The expedition was at a disadvantage from the beginning. Neither Arnold nor Washington suspected that their maps of the region, which had been drawn by a British army engineer, were woefully incomplete. Furthermore, the two hundred flat-bottomed boats that Arnold had commissioned for the journey had been hastily built from green wood. Heavy and clumsy, they floated so poorly that they were worthless for all but the calmest water.

Arnold's expedition ran into one impassable section of river after another. Be-fore long, it was hopelessly bogged down as the men had to haul their heavy boats through miles of knee-deep mud. Steady rains caused most of their food to spoil, and there was no way for them to get more. On November 1, one member of the party wrote in his journal, "This day I passed a number of soldiers who had no provisions, and some that were sick. . . . One or two dogs were killed, which the distressed soldiers eat with good appetite, even the feet and skins."[19] The delays extended their trip into late autumn, and they had made no provisions for when the weather turned bitterly cold. More than three hundred of the soldiers eventually turned back, and deaths from illness and exposure further eroded Arnold's force.

General Richard Montgomery led an American attempt to take Quebec City from the British.

Daunting Odds

Off to the west, Montgomery finally made some progress. On November 2, after a forty-five-day siege, Fort St. John's finally surrendered, leaving Montreal exposed to attack. Recognizing his poor military position, General Carleton declined further defense of the city, retreating instead to Quebec City. On November 13, the American forces accomplished the first of

Benedict Arnold: Hero and Traitor

The leader of the American expedition to Quebec was perhaps the most promising young military officer in the army. Born on January 14, 1741, Benedict Arnold came from a respected family and was the great-grandson of the first governor of Rhode Island. After his alcoholic father squandered the family fortune, the enterprising Arnold went into business on his own. By the age of twenty-one, he owned one of the more prosperous pharmacies in the colonies.

At the start of the Revolutionary War, Arnold obtained a commission as captain. Upon hearing that the Americans needed cannons to drive the British army out of Boston, he hatched a scheme to get them by capturing British forts on Lake Champlain. He gained authorization for this, but then found that another group headed by Ethan Allen had been sent to do the same thing. The headstrong Arnold caught up to Allen and through considerable wrangling worked out a deal whereby they jointly led the successful assault of Fort Ticonderoga.

Arnold's fearless and inspiring leadership in Quebec and at Saratoga earned him high praise from his troops and from historians. Had he been killed instead of just wounded at Saratoga, he would have been remembered as a Patriot hero, and schools and other public buildings would be named after him today.

But his hot temper, aggressive nature, and record of success got him in continual trouble with other jealous American officers, particularly his superior, Horatio Gates. Gates did not even mention Arnold's crucial role in the Saratoga campaign in his reports to Congress. Rather than praise Arnold, Congress questioned his expenditures on the Quebec campaign and then refused to reimburse him. Arnold was furious.

His severe leg wound at Bemis Heights prevented him resuming command on the battlefield where he excelled. Through the influence of George Washington, one of his most enthusiastic backers, Arnold obtained a commission as military governor of Philadelphia after the British withdrew from the city. It was not the sort of job at which Arnold excelled. He lived too high and made many enemies, particularly when he married Peggy Shippen, the daughter of a Loyalist. The upshot was that Arnold found himself facing charges of abuse of power. At his trial in February 1779, he was acquitted of all but two minor charges.

But by now, bitterness toward his country consumed him. He had also fallen deeply in debt and wanted the war to be over so he could resume his former career. He managed to convince himself that he would do everyone a favor by betraying his country and ending the war. Arnold got himself assigned to a command of West Point, a key fort protecting the Hudson River. Then he agreed to turn over the fort to the British in exchange for a huge sum of money.

The plot was discovered at the last minute, and Arnold narrowly escaped with his life. With nowhere else to turn, he fought for the British in subsequent action. When the British lost the war, he was forced to spend his life in exile in England. He died there in 1801, miserable and deeply in debt. The man who was a true American hero in 1777 became the most despised man in his homeland. Fellow officer Nathanael Greene wrote of him, quoted in Charles Royster's *A Revolutionary People at War:* "how despised, loved by none, and hated by all. Once his Country's Idol, now her horror." Benedict Arnold's name has since become a synonym for traitor.

their two objectives by occupying Montreal.

At about the same time, Arnold's starving, exhausted troops finally reached the St. Lawrence River opposite Quebec City. The journey had been nearly twice as long as anticipated, covering 350 miles instead of the predicted 180. The brutal conditions that Arnold's men overcame along the way have led historians to rank this as one of the most heroic military marches in history.

Arnold rounded up canoes from local Native Americans and crossed the St. Lawrence at night to avoid the patrolling British warships. But now, with his army reduced to six hundred men, a supply of only five rounds of ammunition per man and no artillery, he faced the prospect of assaulting a heavily walled city guarded by twelve hundred soldiers who knew they were coming and who had spent the past few weeks preparing for the attack. A rumor that the British were about to attack him sent Arnold retreating twenty miles to the west to rest and await reinforcements.

Having left enough men to secure Montreal, Montgomery joined Arnold on December 2, along with 350 men, badly needed provisions (including winter uniforms captured at Montreal), and cannons. In the meantime, though, Carleton and his men reached Quebec City, swelling its defenses to eighteen hundred, compared to roughly one thousand Americans. Conventional military wisdom says that an army attacking an entrenched opponent should outnumber its foe by two-to-one to have a

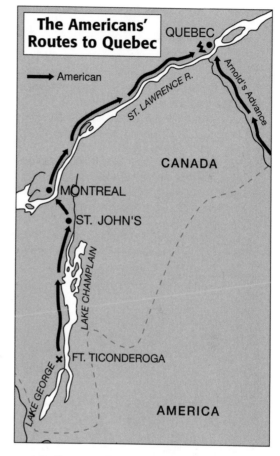

good chance of success. Yet, undaunted by the odds, Montgomery and Arnold arrived at Quebec City on December 5 and brazenly demanded its surrender. When the British ignored them, the siege began. On December 10, the American forces approached from the west along the plains high above the river to within seven hundred yards of the city and began firing their largest guns. To their dismay, their largest cannon balls merely bounced off the thick walls of the fortress city, and the Americans had to call off the attack.

Quebec—Key to Canada

Because of its strategic location on the St. Lawrence River, the waterway into the heart of Canada, Quebec was the site of more campaigns of conquest than any other city in North America. It was the site of the Indian village of Stadacona when the French explorer Jacques Cartier became the first European to visit the region in 1535. In 1608, Samuel de Champlain founded the city of Quebec on the site. Although it contained only a handful of residents, the British took the town from the French in 1629, but returned it three years later. Two later British expeditions to capture the city, in 1690 and 1711, ended in failure. In 1759, Quebec was the site of the most important battle of the Seven Years' War. After being thrown back with heavy losses in his ini-

tial assault, British general James Wolfe learned of a secret trail that brought his army near the walls of the city before they were detected. In the bitter fighting that followed, Wolfe was killed. But the British captured the city and in so doing dealt a crippling blow to French interests in North America.

At the time of the American invasion, Quebec had been in British hands for only sixteen years. It had grown to a city of more than fifteen hundred houses and was easily the largest population center in Canada.

Quebec City as it was seen from Pointe Levy in 1761, two years after being captured from the French by the British.

As Montgomery and Arnold probed for some weakness in the city, time began to turn against them. The Americans never dreamed the invasion would take so long, and now the term of enlistment for most of their soldiers was up at the end of the month. Other than the addition of a few disgruntled Canadians, they could expect

no reinforcements. Somehow they had to pull off a victory in the next three weeks.

A Dark and Stormy Night

Quebec City consisted of two parts, the Upper Town and the Lower Town; Arnold and Montgomery finally decided that the Lower Town was the most vulnerable part of the city and planned to attack it from two sides. Montgomery's force would approach from the west, along the river, while Arnold and his troops attacked the entrance known as the Palace Gate from the north. The two forces would meet in the middle of the Lower Town's business district and then force their way up the main road to Upper Town. In order to shield their movements from the enemy and catch them unprepared, they planned to attack at night, during a snowstorm.

Time nearly ran out on the Americans as they waited for the right weather. Cold and disgruntled, most of the troops were ready to give up the venture and go home. In an attempt to stoke their enthusiasm, Mongomery promised the troops they could plunder the city once they occupied it.

At last, on the night of December 30, a major snowstorm blew in. The Americans moved into position with great difficulty, especially Montgomery's men, who had to struggle down the icy slopes along the river through ice, snow, and howling wind, with no light to guide them. But at 4 A.M., Montgomery fired rockets signaling to Arnold the start of the attack.

Unfortunately for the Americans, the rockets also alerted Carleton, who knew exactly what the Americans were doing, thanks to a Rhode Island deserter who had revealed the plan to him just the day before. Montgomery was surprised to find no resistance when he reached the west edge of town. His men overran two barricades that had been left undefended and approached

a third that seemed likewise abandoned. The defenders appeared to have been caught completely unawares, which may have accounted for Montgomery's lack of caution when he strode forward with his top aide and a battalion commander to check out the barricade. They walked right into an ambush. From point blank range, the hidden defenders fired their only load of cannon shot and their muskets as well, killing all three American leaders. Command fell

Benedict Arnold took a musket ball in the leg during the storming of the Palace Gate in Quebec City.

to Lieutenant Colonel Donald Campbell, who lost his nerve and immediately called off the attack.

Verge of a Miracle

On the other end of town, Arnold was having better luck. He and his men managed to get past the cannons guarding the Palace Gate with few losses. They ran some six hundred yards, dodging fire from the walls above, and hurled themselves at a manned barricade. There the impetuous Arnold, who had insisted on leading the charge himself, took a musket ball in the leg and had to

be carried back to safety. Command then fell to Daniel Morgan who, unlike Campbell, was every bit as aggressive as the man he replaced.

Under Morgan's direction, the Americans raced forward, smashing all resistance and taking scores of prisoners along the way. As they had hoped, they received some assistance from French citizens of the city, who shouted, "Vive la liberte!" [20] The city's British defenders appeared confused and scared. Morgan found the main barricade that guarded the street to Upper Town undefended. Despite the disaster on the west end

Daniel Morgan—Fearless Rifleman

Only the desperate pleading of his fellow officers persuaded Daniel Morgan not to go down fighting in the streets of Quebec. It was not the first time that this man of legendary toughness had defied death.

Morgan had been fighting in wars off and on since he had joined a French and Indian War expedition as a teamster at the age of nineteen. A man of intense pride, he committed the crime of striking a British officer who struck him with the flat of his sword in 1756. Morgan survived his punishment of two hundred lashes, stoking his thirst for revenge against the British. A few years later, he lost all of his teeth when a ball from an Indian's musket struck him in the neck and passed through his mouth.

At the start of the war, Morgan received a commission as captain of a regiment of Virginia riflemen. After his reluctant surrender at Quebec, he languished in a jail in that city until the following summer, when he was released in a prisoner exchange. In 1777, he joined Washington's army. That fall, Washington sent him to reinforce General Gates against Burgoyne. Like Arnold, Morgan ran afoul of Gates. Not only did Gates neglect to cite his

contributions in that campaign, but he made Morgan pay for refusing to support Gates's bid to oust Washington as overall commander of the Continental army. Morgan could not get a promotion to a command after that. He spent the memorable winter of 1778–1779 at Valley Forge but then resigned from the army in disgust on July 18, 1779.

Morgan, however, did not have the temperament to sit on the sidelines. According to Robert Coakley and Stetson Conn in *The War of the American Revolution,* after the terrible defeat of Gates's army at Camden, South Carolina, "he put aside his personal grievances and hastened to join Gates at Hillsboro." His services were desperately needed at this time, and he had no problem being advanced to general and given command of a portion of the American army in the South. He led the American army in its stunning defeat of the British at Cowpens (see chapter 7) before resigning again due to poor health in 1781. Morgan was as successful in civilian life as he was as a general. By 1796, he owned a quarter million acres of land, and the following year he won election to Congress. Morgan died in 1802.

of town, the Americans had boldly fought their way to the verge of an astounding victory.

Morgan's Hesitation

But as Morgan urged his men forward, he met with resistance from his officers, who reminded him that the plan was to meet with Montgomery before proceeding into Upper Town. Also, Arnold and Morgan had led the attack at such a furious pace that at least a third of their force had been unable to keep up. After losing contact with their comrades, they had gotten lost in the city's confusing maze of streets. Morgan's men were also in the dangerous position of being outnumbered by the prisoners they had taken.

Reluctantly, Morgan agreed to wait for Montgomery and try to locate his lost soldiers. The decision proved disastrous. As Morgan later lamented, "I gave up my own opinion and lost the town."[21] The delay stopped the Americans' momentum and allowed the panicked defenders to calm down and regroup. Carleton took advantage of the lull to position soldiers in key spots throughout the city, including a previously unguarded barricade protecting Upper Town.

When dawn arrived and Montgomery still had not appeared, Morgan finally resumed the assault. Although they fought with skill and determination, the Americans now faced impossible odds. British soldiers hidden in houses fired at them from every angle. For most of the day, the Americans struggled to advance, still looking over their shoulders for reinforcements from Mont-

Sir Guy Carleton commanded the British forces defending Quebec City.

gomery. Finally, realizing that their cause was hopeless, they retreated back through town, only to find that a barricade they had thought to be deserted was now manned by two hundred British soldiers. Cut off from retreat, the American force disintegrated into scattered pockets of resistance. Most of the attackers were surrounded and captured, including Morgan.

The Americans suffered 60 casualties in the assault, and another 426 were captured. British losses in the battle were only 5 killed and 13 wounded. Arnold escaped capture only because Carleton pulled back his forces before they could reach the American hospital. Including Montgomery's forces, some six hundred American soldiers escaped the debacle.

American Stubbornness

Incredibly, Arnold refused to abandon his mission. "I have no thought of leaving this proud town until I enter it in triumph,"[22] he insisted. All winter long, the Americans huddled in misery on the outskirts of Quebec, hoping for reinforcements. Arnold lost any chance of fulfilling his goal, however, when the slow healing of his leg wound and his frustration with his lack of supplies and manpower forced him to turn over his field command and accept reassignment to the relative comfort of Montreal.

His fellow Americans, however, proved nearly as stubborn as Arnold in their obsession with Quebec. In the spring of 1776, nearly six thousand colonial soldiers marched up from New York and Massachusetts into Canada. However, British general John Burgoyne arrived in Quebec at about the same time with a relief force of four thousand British soldiers and German mer-

General Richard Montgomery is cut down in an ambush as he approached a barricade that had seemed deserted.

cenaries called Hessians. On June 8, the British ambushed a large American force near Trois-Rivières, halfway between Montreal and Quebec. The Americans were so badly mauled in the fighting that they pulled out of Canada two weeks later, never to return during the war.

Close Call

The invasion of Canada was the Americans' most ambitious undertaking of the war. Due to the courage of leaders such as Arnold, Morgan, and Montgomery, the expedition came close to succeeding despite heavy odds against it and one terrible stroke of misfortune after another. Whether or not the Americans could have held on to their gains against Burgoyne's relief force is debatable. But had they done so, the Americans would not have had to deal with the British invasion from the north that came in the following year. Given the eventual success of the revolution, American control of Canada throughout the war could well have meant that the nation known as the United States would have included a large section of what is now Canada.

Chapter 3

Trenton

he humiliation of having their army chased out of Boston stirred the British government into aggressive action. During the summer of 1776, they outfitted a huge military force, powerful enough, they believed, to crush the upstart colonials once and for all. More than four hundred ships set sail for America, carrying over thirty-two thousand well-equipped soldiers. Their attention initially was focused on the important seaport of New York. Opposing them were more than twenty thousand American soldiers under the command of General George Washington. Recognizing the importance of New York City to the American cause, Washington had concentrated his forces in that area.

Collapse of the American Military in New York

The colonial soldiers, despite their lack of training, inexperience, and youth (half were under the age of eighteen), were confident to the point of cockiness. While not nearly as well supplied as the British, many of the colonials were equipped with rifles, as opposed to the standard British muskets, and believed this gave them a huge advantage. Rifles were far more accurate than muskets, especially at long range, and given the British strategy of marching in formation toward the enemy, the Americans believed they could continue to pick them off at will as they had at Bunker Hill.

They failed to take into account an important flaw in the rifle: unlike the musket, it could not be fitted with a bayonet. Americans had little liking for bayonets, and considered them a barbaric form of fighting. But in the battles around New York, they discovered what a terrifying weapon bayonets could be.

With their invincible navy giving them absolute control over the waterways, the British were able to outmaneuver the colonial forces time and again around New York. Washington, who had never distinguished himself as a military leader in any action up to this point, compounded his problems with his hesitant and stumbling leadership. On August 27, Washington allowed his British opponent, General William Howe, to outflank his army at Long Island, with the result that the American forces were completely routed. In this battle and others, the dreaded Hessian mercenaries performed such murderous work with their bayonets that the colonials' confidence evaporated overnight. The very sight of Hessian troops could throw the untrained and undisciplined American troops into panic. At one point, Washington fumed about his troops, "Good God! Are these the men with whom I am to defend America?"[23]

Washington made an even greater mistake at Fort Washington. Recognizing the British advantage in numbers, firepower, and water transportation, Washington saw that the fort was virtually indefensible. However, since he was not actually present at the fort, he did not want to impose his views on those in charge. He allowed the energetic young general Nathanael Greene to persuade him that the fort could be held.

Instead the Americans suffered perhaps their greatest disaster of the war. The

After a disastrous defeat at the Battle of Long Island, American soldiers suffered from low morale and a fear of Hessian troops.

British surrounded the fort and attacked on November 16. So demoralized and out-generaled were the American defenders that they barely put up a fight. After a brief clash in which only twelve of their number were killed, the Americans fled back to the fort, where they huddled in fear and then surrendered. Having barely broken a sweat and with virtually no sacrifice of men, the British bagged twenty-eight hundred prisoners. Washington himself needed a miracle to extract himself and his army from almost certain destruction.

On the Verge of Defeat

The string of disasters in New York shattered morale in Washington's army and left him scrambling for survival. "If I were to wish the bitterest curse to an enemy on this side of the grave, I should put him in my stead with my feelings," [24] said Washington. His once-confident soldiers, so eager to join the fight for freedom after the success at Bunker Hill, immediately saw the error of their ways. The British army was the best-trained army in the world, and the ragtag American army seemed hopelessly outclassed. Nearly half of Washington's army left the service and went back to their homes. Washington pleaded for help from the New Jersey militia, which had boasted a strength of seventeen thousand men. But suddenly, there were few militia to be found. When arrogant General Charles Lee disregarded Washington's or-

Escape from Brooklyn Heights

No man was more important to the eventual success of the American Revolution than Continental army commander George Washington. On at least three occasions, Washington came perilously close to being either killed or captured, but he managed to escape each time by the narrowest of margins.

The first occasion came during the disastrous campaign to defend New York in the summer of 1776. A series of strategic errors and military defeats had placed Washington and nearly ten thousand troops in an impossible situation at Brooklyn Heights. A British force of more than fifteen thousand had pinned them with their backs to the East River. At that point the British fleet was poised to sail up the river unchallenged and complete the trap of the Americans. But rather than risk a bloody frontal attack, British general Howe opted to bring in heavy artillery to finish the job.

Heavy rains, however, delayed the effort, and in the meantime, Washington came to understand the danger he was in. On August 28, as the British placed their siege artillery batteries within six hundred yards of the American lines, he made plans to flee. Realizing the danger he would be in if the British caught him trying to cross the river, he told no one of his plans to evacuate until the order was given on the night of August 29.

The withdrawal would have been an utter disaster had the British fleet sailed on schedule and come upon the fleeing army. But on the night of the twenty-ninth, a storm came up that kept the ships from sailing. Then, just as the Americans were most vulnerable to attack from Howe's army, the winds miraculously shifted. A small but dense pocket of fog settled on the east side of the river, shielding Washington's movements from the British. Washington's men moved so quickly and quietly that by the time the fog lifted in midmorning and the British advanced, virtually his entire army and all but six of his artillery pieces were safely across the river.

der to bring his army southward to join him, Washington found himself in deep trouble.

Desperately, Washington and his dwindling army fled south toward Pennsylvania, with a vastly superior British force under General Cornwallis in hot pursuit. Colonial America's sense of doom was so overpowering that Washington's troops had difficulty finding citizens who would sell them food or let them sleep in their barns. To make matters worse, the enlistments of two thousand of Washington's men were up at the end of the month, and they declined to rejoin. The main American army that had stood at twenty thousand earlier that summer had now shrunk to three thousand. Of the one hundred cannons with which they had started the summer, they retained only a dozen.

But Washington had learned an important lesson from the New York fiasco. His army was no match for the British in a lengthy, full-scale engagement. In order for his army to survive—and survive it must if the revolution was to succeed—he had to begin fighting a different kind of war. "We will never seek a protracted action," he declared. "We will protract the war."[25] Washington's new plan was always to lurk close enough to threaten the British forces but still avoid a decisive confrontation.

General Charles Lee (pictured) ignored Washington's order to bring his army south.

The strategy began to frustrate the British immediately. Washington stayed tantalizingly close, but whenever the British tried to engage him in battle, he slipped away. Time after time, Washington would slip out of a town just before the British arrived. One of Howe's officers complained: "They will neither fight nor totally run away. But they keep at such a distance that we are

always a day's march from them. We seem to be playing at Bo-Peep."[26]

American Army at Low Ebb

In early December, however, the British seemed to have cornered Washington and his small army at last. The Americans had nowhere to go but south toward the Delaware River, and once they reached that, they would be stuck. Cornwallis was convinced that Washington could not hope to get his force across the Delaware before the British arrived to capture them.

Yet once again, Washington evaded capture. The American general managed to

Washington had a knack for quickly moving the American army as he demonstrated in the retreat from Long Island in 1776.

ferry his entire force across the river in boats. But while they were disappointed at the American escape, the British were not worried. As far as they were concerned, the American military effort was finished. How long could even these men last, given the fact that the Continental Congress had not even provided them with tents with which to shelter themselves during the winter?

Confident that the Americans posed no threat, the British hunkered down to wait for spring to come before finishing them off. So disdainful were they of the Americans that they felt free to disperse their army in garrisons throughout New Jersey to protect Loyalist Americans from Patriot raids rather than keeping the army concentrated in one place. In the words of historian W. J. Wood, "Howe and Cornwallis obviously felt nothing but contempt for an enemy who, they believed, was not only incapable of mounting a winter offensive but who would, in all probability, not be able to survive the winter as a force to be reckoned with." [27]

At this stage, Washington realized the revolution was on its last legs. Even when he was joined by three thousand soldiers of the Pennsylvania militia, and Continental troops under the command of Sullivan, he had fewer than five thousand able-bodied soldiers, facing an enemy with three times that number. Of the troops Washington had at his disposal, the vast majority had enlisted for only a year, and that year would be up at the end of December, in just a few weeks. In a gloomy mood, Washington wrote to his brother Augustine, "Our dependence now is on the speedy inlistment of a New Army; if this fails us I think the game is pretty nearly up. . . ." [28]

A Daring Plan

Despite his desperate position, Washington felt obligated to try a daring move to try and salvage public morale. If he could not, the Americans had no hope of assembling and keeping an army, and the war would be over. As Washington later said, his reason for formulating an attack in his army's weakened condition was "as much owing to the want of army to look the Enemy in the face, as to any other cause." [29]

Washington came up with the bold plan of recrossing the Delaware River in midwinter and attacking three of the most important British supply stores in New Jersey. First, he would hit Trenton, then move up to Princeton, and finally strike New Brunswick—and then dash away before the British could catch him. Washington planned to risk his entire army in the attack. He would lead the main force of

In the winter of 1776, General John Sullivan led three thousand soldiers to augment Washington's struggling army.

twenty-four hundred in a nighttime crossing of the Delaware upstream, nine miles north of Trenton. They would then march on Trenton and before dawn attack the fourteen-hundred-man Hessian force stationed there.

Meanwhile, Lieutenant Colonel John Cadwalader would cross downstream with nineteen hundred men and attack the Hessian force at Brodentown as a diversion. Finally, General James Ewing was to cross the river just south of Trenton with seven hundred men and hold a key bridge to seal off any Hessian escape from Trenton.

Washington confided the plan to General Gates, a man with more military experience than Washington, who thought it was completely unworkable. But Washington had learned another lesson in New York: if he was to succeed, he needed to establish his leadership without worrying about the feelings of subordinates. Upon hearing Gates's

The First Crossing of the Delaware

Few events of the Revolutionary War are more celebrated than Washington's crossing of the Delaware River in the dead of winter. But while most tales of this event centered on the Battle of Trenton, Washington's first crossing while fleeing from the British army was perhaps even more significant.

With his militia deserting at an alarming rate after the defeats in New York in the fall of 1776, Washington's ragged, tiny army was no match for the British that pursued him. Realizing this, General Cornwallis pursued Washington aggressively in hopes of finishing him off. On November 28, Cornwallis's troops nearly caught Washington as he was leaving Newark. In desperation, Washington raced southward with Cornwallis close on his heels. Benson Bobrick, in *Angel in the Whirlwind,* quotes Washington admitting to one of his generals that the fact that he had not been caught yet was "more owing to the badness of the weather than to any resistance we could make."

As the armies approached the Delaware River, both Washington and Cornwallis knew that the Americans were in serious trouble. There was no bridge available in the area. There appeared to be no way for Washington to get his army across the river in boats before Cornwallis arrived to destroy him.

Fortunately for Washington, he remembered once seeing a fleet of huge cargo boats, known as Durham boats, on the river at Philadelphia. These boats, which were up to sixty feet long, were used to haul iron—up to fifteen tons per load—in shallow water. Washington sent men on his fastest horses ahead with orders to get these boats at all costs and have them sent upriver to where he needed to cross. They were also to destroy all other boats on the river.

By the time Washington's army arrived at the river on December 5, twenty-five to thirty of the giant boats were ready and waiting. Washington loaded his army, forty to fifty on a boat, together with his equipment and supplies. To his great fortune, his army included a regiment of sailors from the Massachusetts coast who were able to man the great boats for the crossing.

Cornwallis, who had expected to finish off Washington on the banks of the river, reached the Delaware only to find his quarry had disappeared. Furthermore, there were no boats to be found on the river, and so the British had no way of continuing the chase. Washington had pulled off another miracle. Had these unusual boats not been available, or had Washington not happened to be aware of them, the war might well have ended on the Delaware shore.

George Washington crosses the Delaware River to surprise the Hessians at Trenton.

objections, Washington dismissed him from command. Gates went to Philadelphia, where he expressed to Congressional leaders his doubts about Washington and openly lobbied for his job. He even told friends that at Trenton, he had given the general enough rope to hang himself.

The Plan Unravels

Washington planned the attack for Christmas night, hoping to catch the Hessians complacent from celebrating the holiday. He ordered his men to pack three days' supply of food and report to the riverside. At about 8 P.M. they boarded the huge boats that had ferried them across the river previously. Washington had hoped to get across early in the night and attack before dawn, but the weather did not cooperate. Freezing rain and snow and blustery winds

hampered the crossing, as did the large ice chunks floating down the river.

Nonetheless, Washington felt he had no choice but to continue. He sent a message to Cadwalader: "I am determined, as the night is favorable, to cross the River and make the attack upon Trenton in the Morning. If you can do nothing real, at least create as great a diversion as possible."[30]

As they shoved off from shore, the swift current pulled the boats downstream and forced the men to pole back against the current. That Washington's men made it across under such conditions is a testament to his leadership skills and to the raw determination of his men. Despite such a woeful lack of clothing that some soldiers had nothing on their feet but cloth wrappings, they braved the brutal, treacherous conditions. Washington not only got his army across, but also his horses and eighteen field artillery pieces.

Such a valiant effort seemed to have been wasted when the timing and element of surprise on which the venture depended began unraveling. Because of the problems with the current, the crossing had taken three hours longer than Washington had estimated, which dashed his hope of attacking Trenton before daybreak. Furthermore, neither Cadwalader nor Ewing had fulfilled his assignment. Cadwalader had managed to get most of his men across, but when conditions were too hazardous for him to get his artillery across, he gave up the venture rather than advance without the big guns. Ewing had not even tried to cross, assuming that it was foolish to even try in such conditions. Even worse, a British sympathizer had observed the American crossing and had informed the Hessians in Trenton.

So as Washington began the nine-mile march to Trenton, his desperate gamble had little chance of succeeding. He would now have to attack a better trained and equipped army that knew he was coming, in broad daylight with exhausted troops, and with no support from his right wing.

Saved by a Mystery

Washington was saved by a mysterious sequence of events that has never been fully explained. About two hours before Wash-

ington's boats landed on the eastern shore, a small group of Americans attacked Trenton from the west—in exactly the point where Washington intended to attack. Although the attackers have never been identified, historians speculate that they may have been a group of perhaps two dozen farmers upset at the treatment they had received from the invaders. Apparently, they had no other goal than to cause whatever mischief they could. At any rate, the attack was easily driven off.

The Hessian commander at Trenton, Colonel Rall, had so little respect for the colonial military that he had earlier declined to carry out orders to build defensive works around the city. "Let them come! We want no trenches," he had boasted. "We'll use the bayonet."[31] This same arrogance led him to assume that this minor skirmish was the attack of which he had been warned. Having defeated it with virtually no effort, he relaxed his guard and gave many of his sentries time off to celebrate the holiday. When further reports arrived of American troops on the east side of the river, Rall dismissed them. He refused to believe the Americans posed any threat at all.

Washington received another break when, again unknown to him, another group of New Jersey militia had made a raid on British positions southeast of Trenton. In response, the Hessian force in the best position to reinforce the troops at Trenton had been sent to deal with the raiders. That meant that Washington did not really need Cadwalader's presence in the area after all.

Surprise Attack

General Greene commanded the left half of Washington's force in a march inland while General Sullivan led the right in an advance along the river. Both units reached the outskirts at 8 A.M., a remarkably precise bit of coordination given the conditions. The sight of a mob of soaked, half-naked, mud-covered, screaming soldiers unnerved the Hessians on the perimeter, and they put up almost no resistance. The main body of Hessians in town was slow to respond. Be- fore they quite realized what was happen- ing, the Americans had swept through the town and placed cannons on a rise that dominated the two main streets.

Because of the freezing rain, neither side could keep its powder dry enough to fire their muskets with any consistency. Fighting was reduced to bayonets, can- nons, and occasional musket fire from houses where soldiers found dry refuge for firing their weapons. Rall made a brave, be- lated attempt to rally his command and

Hessians: Hired Guns of the British Army

The British government had so many military interests around the world that it had great difficulty recruiting enough soldiers to meet its requirements. As a result, they sought foreign professional soldiers whom they could hire to fight for them. But rather than attempting to re- cruit individual foreigners, they signed treaties in which they agreed to pay the foreign nation for the services of large numbers of soldiers. At first, the British tried to negotiate terms for twenty thousand soldiers from Russia but were unsuc- cessful. They then turned to German princes who had no qualms about selling the services and the lives of their subjects in exchange for silver. The first treaty involving the purchase of German soldiers to combat the American Revo- lution took place on January 9, 1776. The cal- lousness of this policy is highlighted by the fact that terms of one treaty offered reimbursement of thirty-five pounds for every soldier killed.

Eventually more than twenty-nine thousand German soldiers, commonly referred to as Hes- sians, sailed to the United States to fight Britain's war. While some of these units were experienced career soldiers, others were reluctant draftees. One Hessian who was being abducted by re- cruiters claimed this was a common occurrence.

In *The Hessians,* Edward J. Lowell quoted him as saying, "No one was safe from the grip of these sellers of souls. Persuasion, cunning, deception, force—all served. Strangers of [all] kinds were ar- rested, imprisoned, sent off."

As a result of the varied backgrounds of the troops, the Hessian units were not equally adept. Lowell quoted General Burgoyne as describing his Hessians as "dispirited and ready to club their arms at the first fire." In general, though, the Hes- sians fought well, and, as Lowell states, "on few occasions during the war did the Hessian sol- diers show either a want of courage or a want of discipline." In fact, their performance in the early battles in New York was so ruthless and efficient that the American militia began to fear them; some units fled at the news that Hessians were approaching.

Only 17,300 Hessians returned to Germany at the end of the war. While some of those who stayed behind were deserters, in general, Amer- icans so feared and hated the Hessians that their numbers were no greater than the number of British army deserters who stayed in America. While some of the twelve thousand Hessians unaccounted for died in battle, most probably died of illness during their tour of duty.

form a bayonet charge to regain the town. But the devastating cannon fire drove the Hessians from the streets, and they fell back to an orchard just outside of town. There, Rall was killed by American musket fire.

Meanwhile, Greene sent two divisions circling around to the north to his left to cut off the Hessians' escape. The Hessians frantically plunged into the river and ran off across country in small groups. Perhaps five hundred of them made it to safety. However, the Americans captured nine hundred of them, along with a great store of artillery, ammunition, and supplies. While twenty-two Hessians were killed in the fighting, not a single American died from battle wounds.

Pushing Their Luck

Having succeeded beyond his wildest dreams, Washington recrossed the Delaware before the British could organize a counterattack. Conditions during this crossing were even worse than they had been the previous night. Three men died of exposure, and one thousand men reported sick the following day.

Regretting his timidity in failing to support Washington, Cadwalader tried to redeem himself by making a belated move across the river. There, he found the British forces in a state of confusion, so he urged Washington to join him in pressing the attack. Despite the ordeal that his men

Washington rallies his men to victory at Trenton.

had gone through, Washington got them to cross the icy river one more time. One of his officers observed that the men were willing to risk the crossing one more time "owing to the impossibility of being in a worse condition than the present one, and therefore the men always liked to be kept moving in expectation of bettering themselves."[32]

On January 2, British general Cornwallis returned with a force of six thousand men and caught up to Washington late in the afternoon. Believing he had trapped the American leader, Cornwallis put off plans to attack until morning. In doing so, he went against the advice of his officers. "If

Colonel Rall surrenders his sword to Washington at the Battle of Trenton.

Washington is the general I take him to be," warned one, "his army will not be found there in the morning."[33]

Sure enough, Washington and his troops silently slipped away during the night and rejoined Cadwalader near Princeton. There, Washington personally led a charge to rout a British force, inflicting 86 casualties and capturing 323 more prisoners at a loss of only 40 killed and wounded. Again, Washington then slipped away before the exasperated Cornwallis could strike him.

So shocked were the British by their defeat that they abandoned their plan of occupying New Jersey and retreated to New York. The American militias, which had been nearly disbanded, returned with renewed spirit.

Washington had taken an outrageous gamble in going on the attack against a superior enemy with an army that was disintegrating. Had he been defeated at Trenton or Princeton, organized military resistance to Britain likely would have ended. Having succeeded, Washington revived an army that had been all but destroyed and made it a force to be reckoned with. In the opinion of the British historian George Trevelyan, "It may be doubted whether so small a number of men ever employed so short a space of time with greater or more lasting results upon the history of the world."[34]

Chapter 4

Saratoga

While yielding command of the British forces in Boston to Generals Howe and Gage in the early stages of the Revolution, General John Burgoyne had spent his time pondering the best way to put down the rebellion. A man prone to grand ambitions, he developed an elaborate and impressive scheme to conduct the war.

It was Burgoyne's belief that New England was the key source of traitorous feelings toward the British government, and his plan sought to isolate this region from the rest of the colonies. This could be done by making use of the Hudson River–Lake Champlain waterway that ran north and south along western New York. Burgoyne proposed sending an army up the Hudson from New York City to meet up with another army coming south from Canada to seal off New England.

Burgoyne Readies His Offensive

Burgoyne had gained an enthusiastic response to his strategy from his superiors in the British government prior to being sent to Quebec in May 1776 with a large relief force to thwart American hopes of conquering Canada. He then returned to London over the winter to flesh out the details of his plan. The government rewarded him for his initiative by giving him command of the British forces in Canada, replacing General Guy Carleton.

Burgoyne returned to Canada in the spring of 1777, eager to begin his expedition. His plan had grown even more grand in recent months and now called for three separate campaigns. Burgoyne himself would lead the main force of forty-two hundred seasoned British soldiers and four thousand professional German troops from the north. An army of eight hundred regular soldiers plus Canadian militia and Indian allies would head east along the Mohawk River valley from Lake Ontario under the command of Lieutenant Colonel Barry St. Leger. Both groups would collect American Loyalists as well as Indians to fight under the

Valcour Island and the Disposable Fleet

Benedict Arnold suffered a one-sided defeat in the 1776 Battle of Valcour Island, but it may have been his most valuable contribution to the American cause. Had he not thrown together a makeshift navy, British commander Guy Carleton likely would have driven down through the Hudson River valley and linked up with Howe. Not even the wily Washington could have coped long against the combined forces of Howe and Carleton.

Carleton began his drive south in midsummer with an army of nearly eleven thousand men. He was slowed, however, by the need for a fleet of ships for the trip down Lake Champlain to the Hudson River. The British completely dismantled an eighteen-gun ship, carried it overland, and began reassembling it at the lake. At the same time, they constructed nearly two dozen smaller warships.

To combat this invasion, Arnold took on a frantic construction effort of his own. Going over the heads of his superiors, he attracted hundreds of carpenters with offers of lucrative pay to build as many ships as possible.

On October 11, the British fleet finally sailed down the lake with more than two dozen warships. Even with their exhausting efforts, the American fleet of sixteen ships was vastly inferior to the British. But Arnold ambushed them and slugged it out with the British for seven hours. Eventually the British got the upper hand and neared total victory as darkness fell. Having cornered the American fleet, they waited for morning to finish them off. Somehow Arnold took advantage of the fog and darkness to slip away from the British. When morning arrived and the British discovered what had happened, they gave chase and caught up later that day. Arnold fought a fierce running battle against his pursuers but finally had to beach most of his ships and burn them to prevent them from falling into enemy hands. Only five of the sixteen American ships returned to safety. Carrying his wounded on sails, Arnold and his men eluded capture and marched twenty miles south to Fort Ticonderoga.

While the Valcour Island was a clear British victory, the battle delayed the British long enough that Carleton decided not to risk continuing his expedition into possible bad weather. He retreated into Canada to try again in the spring, giving the Americans time they needed to regroup.

banner as they went. The two forces would meet at Albany, New York, and then head south to link up with General Howe's army coming up from New York City. Burgoyne had no fear of the American forces, which he termed "a preposterous parade of military arrangement."[35] He believed that any American army that tried to stop him would be caught between his three converging armies and destroyed. Burgoyne was so pleased with his plan that he made a sizable bet with a friend that he would defeat the Americans and be back in England within a year.

Flaws in the Scheme

Burgoyne's scheme, which had looked so convincing on paper, proved to be riddled with flaws. The Canadians were not interested in going south to fight for the British against the Americans. Instead of the anticipated two thousand Canadian militia, the expedition was able to recruit only 150. Similarly, only four hundred Indians took up arms with the British, rather than the expected two thousand. That left St. Leger's force dangerously thin. Burgoyne would soon discover that his optimism about the strength of the Loyalists in New York had also been vastly overestimated.

Furthermore, the British military was not particularly well trained for wilderness warfare. Their tight formations and disciplined maneuvers were far more suited to clearings and open plains than to bogs, dense forests, and steep, rocky slopes. They also had little experience in keeping supplies flowing to their army in such terrain.

Finally, Burgoyne, despite his ambitions and enormous confidence, was a poor choice to lead a wilderness campaign. Gentleman Johnny, as he was nicknamed, had a strong preference for luxurious living that caused him to burden his campaign with unnecessary supplies and baggage. Such a man was not likely to hold up well in the face of the discomfort and supply shortages that more experienced wilderness fighters took for granted. His loud and boastful manner also tended to create more critics than loyal followers, as did the suspicion that he had gained his high position in the army due to his marriage to a member of the British aristocracy rather than through his abilities.

A Shortcut Nightmare

Despite these weaknesses, the expedition got off to an auspicious start. In the absence of any American navy, Burgoyne was able to advance unchallenged down Lake Champlain. In his first engagement, at Fort Ticonderoga, Burgoyne took advantage of a huge American blunder. General Philip

British general John Burgoyne constructed an elaborate plan to end the Revolution, betting a friend that he could defeat the Americans within a year.

Schuyler had expected his contingent at the fort to put up a strong defense against any assault, but he had neglected the repeated warnings of subordinates that the fort was vulnerable to artillery fired from nearby Mount Defiance. The British found the hill undefended and quickly hauled up their heavy artillery, which they trained on

American general Philip Schuyler ignored warnings that Fort Ticonderoga was vulnerable to artillery fire from Mount Defiance.

the fort. Defenseless against this long-range bombardment, Ticonderoga's defenders had no choice but to abandon the fort without a fight after only a four-day siege. As they made a headlong dash for safety, they were chased and caught by pursuing British under the command of General Simon Fraser. A hard-fought battle followed in which the British and their German mercenaries emerged victorious.

At this point, however, Burgoyne made the kind of crucial mistake that George Washington was astute enough to predict when he commented, "I trust General Burgoyne's army will meet sooner or later with an effectual check and as I suggested before that the success he has had will precipitate his ruin." [36] In order to take advantage of the easiest route to the south, Burgoyne needed to go back up Lake Champlain to Ticonderoga, turn west, and then come down Lake George. This would have brought his army to Fort George, where he could have established a good supply base. From there he could have followed an established road to Fort Edward, on the Hudson River. Burgoyne, however, did not want to retrace his steps. He thought he could save time by taking what appeared to be a shorter route through the wilderness to Fort Edward.

The shortcut proved to be a nightmare. As if the rugged wilderness was not difficult enough for travel, Schuyler set one thousand men to work felling trees in Burgoyne's path. Weighed down by their ponderous baggage, Burgoyne's army managed to cover only seventy-three miles in twenty-one

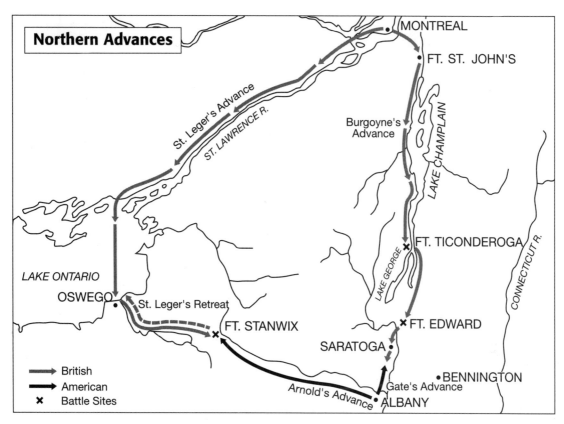

Northern Advances

days and did not reach Fort Edward until July 30. This not only used up valuable supplies and prime traveling weather, it also gave the scattered American forces time to reform their defenses.

Burgoyne's Help Evaporates

At the same time, the other two prongs of the British offensive were disintegrating. To the west, St. Leger's small army was paying the price for the British army's vain reliance on militia and Indians for support. It fell behind schedule as it tried to force the surrender of Fort Stanwix in western New York. St. Leger's ambush of an American

force that was coming to the aid of the fort quickly escalated into a vicious battle that cost him valuable troops. The bloody fighting also disillusioned many of his Indian allies, who abandoned the expedition.

On August 6, the American army facing Burgoyne took a chance and weakened its defenses by sending troops under the command of Benedict Arnold to rescue the fort. Realizing he did not have the manpower to fight Arnold's force, St. Leger had no choice but to give up his entire mission and retreat back to Ontario. Having driven off the western threat, Arnold and his men then returned to confront Burgoyne's army

St. Leger's Retreat

British lieutenant colonel Barry St. Leger had ex- pected few problems on his march from On- tario to link up with General Burgoyne. He was surprised to learn, however, that Fort Stanwix, which the British thought had been abandoned, was occupied by 750 colonials. St. Leger stopped to lay siege to the fort.

Upon hearing that General Nicolas Herkimer was approaching with eight hundred militiamen to relieve the fort, St. Leger prepared an ambush for him at a ravine six miles from the fort. Caught in crossfire from all sides, the Americans suffered terrible initial losses. But instead of surrendering, they regrouped and fought back fiercely at the Battle of Oriskany. Nearly two hundred Americans died in fierce fighting, and they were forced to

turn back without reaching the fort. But the heavy losses they inflicted on the Indians caused them to have second thoughts about continuing the campaign.

Meanwhile, the fort sent out a call for rein- forcements from the Americans confronting Bur- goyne to the east. Benedict Arnold answered the call, forming a volunteer army of eleven hundred men. He sent ahead of him a man to spread ru- mors the Americans were on the way with thou- sands of troops. Upon hearing this, the remaining Indians in St. Leger's command departed. On Au- gust 22, before Arnold arrived, St. Leger decided to call it quits. He headed back to Ontario, taking with him troops upon which Burgoyne had been depending.

before he could take advantage of their ab- sence.

Even worse news arrived from General Howe in mid-August. Not only was St. Leger not coming to Burgoyne's aid, neither was Howe. Actually, Howe had made his inten- tions clear months before when he told the British secretary of state, Lord George Ger- main, that he planned to focus his efforts in 1777 on capturing Philadelphia. There was little chance that he could do that and march up the Hudson River. Yet, despite having approved Burgoyne's plan, Germain also approved Howe's plan, apparently in the belief that Howe would quickly take Philadelphia and return to New York in time to take part in Burgoyne's campaign. But, having received approval for his ac- tions, Howe left a small force at New York City under General Henry Clinton and took his army right out of Burgoyne's grand

scheme. Whether jealousy between Bur- goyne and Howe entered into the picture or whether the fault lay purely in lack of communication, the result was the same: Burgoyne was now on his own.

Bennington

As his glorious strategy began to fall apart, Burgoyne realized that he needed to pay more attention to his supply situation. On August 18, he sent out a group of six hun- dred soldiers under Lieutenant Colonel Friedrich Baum on a raid into the country- side for food and horses. An American force discovered their movements. Before long Baum's men were surrounded near the vil- lage of Bennington, Vermont, by a force double their size, led by one of the colonials' most able generals, John Stark. Stark was not one to let an opportunity slip away. "Tonight the flag flies from that hill or Molly Stark sleeps a widow!"[37] he roared to his men. They responded by crushing Baum's force. Virtually the entire British command was either killed or captured, at a loss of only thirty dead and forty wounded to the Americans.

The terrible defeat stunned Burgoyne. The losses at Bennington reduced his army to around six thousand. General Horatio Gates, who had taken over command of the American army from Schuyler, now outnumbered him, with at least seven thousand men. That number was growing daily as reports of atrocities committed by the British and their Indian allies inspired vengeful recruits.

Burgoyne now faced a critical decision. Should he admit that the situation had changed, that the odds against him were now too great, and abandon the entire enterprise? Or was now the time to exert his leadership, keep going, and find a way to salvage the glorious victory that he sought?

On September 11, he received a letter from General Clinton that persuaded him to keep going. In it, Clinton promised to make "a push at Montgomery in about 10 days."[38] Burgoyne assumed this meant that Clinton was at last going to carry out the original plan and begin his drive up the Hudson River. In that case, Burgoyne was in no particular danger. He needed only to

General John Stark directs troop movements during the Battle of Bennington.

assume a cautious defensive position and wait for Clinton to arrive. He decided to sever his hopelessly stretched lines of supply and communication with Canada and press on to Albany. Clinton, however, had intended something different in his letter. He had no intention of abandoning the New York City area to meet Burgoyne at Albany. His push was meant only as a diversion to scare the Americans into pulling some of their troop strength away from Burgoyne to deal with Clinton.

Freeman's Farm

On September 13, Burgoyne crossed to the west bank of the Hudson at Saratoga and then turned south. Four miles north of Stillwater, he encountered Gates's army entrenched on Bemis Heights. The British had to maneuver carefully to avoid getting caught in an ambush among the narrow passes between the hills and the river. Be-

A wounded Benedict Arnold leads the American attack on Hessian forces at Saratoga.

lieving that he held a strong defensive position, Gates decided to sit back and wait for the British to charge. He had visions of wreaking the kind of destruction on them that the colonial forces had inflicted on the British assault at Bunker Hill.

But General Arnold detected a weakness in the American formation—it was vulnerable to artillery fire from the hills on the left. In a heated argument with Gates that opened a lasting feud, Arnold argued for taking the offensive before the British could exploit that advantage. On September 19, Arnold put his plan into action. As the British cautiously advanced in three columns, Daniel Morgan and his Virginia riflemen charged into the center column. In fierce fighting at a spot known as Freeman's Farm, the battle raged back and forth for three hours. Finally, the Americans began to drive back their foes. Seeing the British lines wavering, Arnold requested reinforcements to seal the victory. Gates not only refused but ordered Arnold to withdraw. Arnold disobeyed the order, but when the German column along the river arrived on the scene, the outgunned Americans were forced to fall back.

As at Bunker Hill, Freeman's Farm was technically a British victory because they held the field at the battle's end. But it was another victory at a price they could not afford to pay. The British suffered twice the casualties of the Americans.

Furious with Arnold's insubordination, Gates gave him no credit for his performance and stripped him of his command.

General Horatio Gates (pictured) blamed the insubordinate General Arnold for the American defeat at Freeman's Farm.

In fact, however, historians believe that Arnold's actions may have saved Gates from disaster. Burgoyne had seen firsthand the folly of the frontal attack at Bunker Hill and had no intention of repeating that mistake. He was moving into position to blast the Americans out of their positions with the forty heavy cannons he had hauled through the wilderness for just that purpose. In the words of historian David McCullough, "If Arnold had gone along with Gates . . . Burgoyne, a far more aggressive general than Carleton, would almost certainly have destroyed Gates' army and seized control of the Hudson River Valley." [39]

Bemis Heights

Instead, his confidence shaken by the mauling his troops took at Freeman's Farm, Burgoyne decided it would be safer to lay low and wait for Clinton to arrive. Accordingly, he halted his march and took up defensive positions.

Clinton did make a threatening move up the Hudson in late September, as he had promised. By October, he had captured Fort Clinton and advanced to within one hundred miles of Albany. But he had no intention of going further, and he might as well have been across the ocean for all the good he did for Burgoyne. Freeman's Farm had depleted Burgoyne's resources while the Americans, sensing that the British were in serious trouble, flocked to Gates's command. By October, reinforcements had brought the American strength to eleven thousand, twice the size of Burgoyne's command. Worse yet, having been stuck in the wilderness far longer than he had intended, Burgoyne was fast running out of food and supplies.

After waiting three weeks for Clinton and with no relief yet in sight, Burgoyne saw that he had to act quickly. Either he must defeat the Americans decisively or retreat. Aggressive by nature, Burgoyne wanted to attack, but he had no clear idea of the American positions or strength. On October 7, he sent Fraser's troops ahead on a probe. They ran into the Americans, who immediately attacked.

Upon hearing the sound of battle, General Arnold could not bear to stay put. As his men cheered him on, he arrived on the scene and again defied orders. He took over command of the attack, and his men quickly overran the British defenders. Fraser retreated and tried to form a second line of defense, but was driven back from there to his army's main defensive line. There, an American attack on a key defensive position failed. But Arnold rode across the battlefield, directly through the crossfire of the two armies, and led a charge from a different angle that was more successful. Arnold paid for his courage by taking another musket ball in the same leg that had been wounded in Quebec. A messenger then arrived from Gates warning Arnold to stay out of the battle, but by then the victory was complete.

The British fared poorly in the wilderness fighting at Bemis Heights, suffering over 600 casualties compared to fewer than 150 for the Americans. To make matters worse, they were forced to abandon their defenses and yield control of the high ground. Burgoyne recognized at last that his plan had failed and attempted a belated retreat to Canada. But, harried by a vastly superior enemy force, he made little progress. At the end of his supplies and with cold weather fast approaching, he was out of options. On October 17, he surrendered his entire army of 5,752 men to Gates at Saratoga, New York.

Burgoyne returned to England in disgrace and was never again trusted to command soldiers. The failure was largely his own fault, beginning with a plan that was unrealistic and poorly coordinated, and that forced British troops into wilderness fighting in which they had little experience and training. Military experts note that Burgoyne's three converging armies were too far apart to be of any use to each other. They could not even communicate effectively, much less coordinate their attacks over such a large area. Their far-flung positions allowed the Americans to concentrate their forces against each individual unit and take them out one by one. In the field, Burgoyne's conduct of the campaign, according to military analyst Craig L. Symonds, was "marred by poor decision-making, hesitancy, and finally, a lack of will." [40]

Native Americans and the Revolution

The Seven Years' War and the American Revolution were both unqualified disasters for the indigenous inhabitants of eastern North America. The French had shown far more consideration than the British for Indian culture and territorial rights, and their expulsion from North America in the Seven Years' War had been a major blow to the Indians. The American colonists, however, were even less respectful than the British of the Indians. They constantly ignored boundaries that the British government tried to maintain between settlers and Indian lands.

Most Indian tribes realized they would be better off under British rule than American and so were susceptible to British persuasion to join their cause. Two of the tribes most affected were the Iroquois in the North and the Cherokee in the South. The Iroquois were a confederation of five tribes centered in western New York. The British counted on them as allies in their invasion from Canada, but the strategy backfired. The murder of a young woman by a group of Indians during the Saratoga campaign triggered a passionate burst of outrage in frontiersmen who then joined up for the militias by the thousands.

Meanwhile, the Iroquois were largely unenthusiastic and unreliable allies. Disagreements over whether to participate in the war split the confederation, with the majority supporting the British and a minority the Americans. When pro-British Iroquois joined Loyalists in a campaign of terror in Pennsylvania, the Americans reacted angrily. In 1779, Washington spent more effort fighting Indians than in fighting the British, sending four thousand troops under General Sullivan on an expedition to Pennsylvania and New York to punish them. According to David Ramsey in *The Life of George Washington*, "The instructions [Washington] gave to General Sullivan were very particular and severe." Aided by Oneida Indians (who were part of the Iroquois confederation), the troops destroyed Indian villages and crops and ruined their land. The Iroquois retaliated against the Oneida that winter. Altogether, so many Iroquois were killed that their population dropped from twelve thousand prior to the war to five thousand at the war's end.

The Cherokee in the South fared no better. Angered by arrogant settlers taking their lands, the Cherokee sided with the British early in the war. This produced an outbreak of violence against them more severe than any directed at the British. After suffering terribly at the hands of Carolina militia, the Cherokee signed a peace treaty in 1777. But clashes between the two peoples continued. Near the end of the war, a colonial military campaign burned fifty Cherokee towns. Historian Anthony Wallace noted in *The Long Bitter Trail: Andrew Jackson and the Indians*, "A legacy of bitterness over atrocities on both sides remained for generations, Western frontiersmen condemning the Indians as murdering savages and the Indians despising the Americans as untrustworthy and brutal."

General Burgoyne surrenders to American forces at Saratoga. The rebel victory led the French to recognize America as an independent nation.

But the fault was not Burgoyne's alone. It was Howe's failure to carry out his part of the plan that doomed Burgoyne in the end, and this was the fault of the British high command. Burgoyne's men were left to their fate by an incompetent strategist in London who was far removed from the reality of war in North America.

Burgoyne's surrender at Saratoga proved to be one of the crucial events of the war. When news of the disastrous British defeat reached France in December of 1777, King Louis XVI's advisers became convinced, for the first time, that the Amer-

icans had a chance to win the war. This in turn persuaded them to support the Americans against France's archenemies from England. On February 6, 1778, France formally recognized the U.S. government. It began sending badly needed money and supplies to support the colonial effort, followed eventually by limited military participation, all of which would play a key role in America's fight for independence.

★ Chapter 5 ★

Brandywine

Building on the surge of optimism produced by his daring victories at Trenton and Princeton and by the flow of French arms and money, Washington began to rebuild his Continental army. His tireless recruiting efforts boosted his command from roughly three thousand at the beginning of 1777 to nearly nine thousand by late spring. It was not clear, however, just what he could do with that army. The experience in New York had taught him the danger of trying to engage the professional British army in full-scale battle.

In late July, Washington received word that General Howe was planning a major new campaign. Leaving a smaller force under Henry Clinton to guard New York City, the British loaded fifteen thousand men on 260 ships and set sail. Washington guessed that Howe's objective was Philadelphia, the colonies' most important city and the seat of the Continental Congress. Much as Washington wanted to avoid a major battle, he believed that he had no choice but to defend Philadelphia for the sake of the nation's morale and to maintain an effective and orderly government.

While Washington began deploying forces for the defense of the city, Howe's

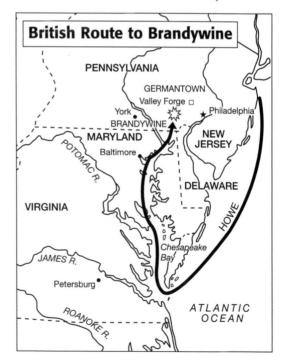

army was doing exactly what Washington had anticipated. His ships sailed up Chesapeake Bay as close as they could get to Philadelphia by sea, and on August 25 they began the short march north to the capital city.

General William Howe prepared a massive British attack on Philadelphia in late 1777.

Preparing to Defend Philadelphia

Washington decided to make his stand along the banks of the Brandywine Creek. The deep and swiftly flowing creek had few bridges and could be crossed at only a limited number of widely spaced fords. That allowed little room for the British to execute their complex maneuvers and forced them to send a thin line of attackers into Americans massed to meet them on the other side. Joined by three thousand members of the Pennsylvania militia, Washington now had more than eleven thousand troops under his command, less than Howe had, but adequate under the circumstances. On September 9, he positioned his troops to cover a six-mile stretch of the Brandywine. He placed Nathanael Greene's division, considered his best, at the likeliest point of attack at Chadds Ford on the main road to Philadelphia, supported by his artillery. He deployed John Sullivan's division on the right in case Howe chose to cross a ford upstream, and he put the militia on his left, where the fords were more difficult.

On September 10, Sullivan expressed concern about his right flank, which would be vulnerable if the British found a nearby ford. At the Battle of Long Island, fought in August of 1776, Howe had caught the Americans flat-footed by outflanking them and had nearly destroyed them. Prodded by Sullivan, Washington asked men in his army who lived in the area if there were any fords further upstream of the northernmost ford under his watch, Buffington's Ford. He was told that there were none within twelve miles.

The Secret Ford

But in this case, despite the fact that the Americans were fighting on their home ground, according to W.J. Wood: "The British had already achieved an advantage. They had been exploiting their reconnaissance capability to the fullest; the Americans had not."[41] From the large concentration of Loyalist farmers in the area, Howe knew where Washington was positioned and roughly the strength of his force. A local Loyalist named Curtis Lewis had given Howe a detailed description of all the fords in the area, including Jeffries Ford, which was two miles north of Buffington's Ford, and was unknown to the American army.

Finding the ford unguarded, Howe made plans to repeat his success at Long Island. He would leave seven thousand men under General Knyphausen to advance to Chadds Ford, while eight thousand men under General Cornwallis crossed at Jeffries Ford, eight miles to the north, and surprised the Americans from the rear.

At 4 A.M. of September 11, Cornwallis began his flanking march. Strangely, instead of marching swiftly to maximize the surprise, Howe insisted on hauling along his heavy cannons with him on the march. The effort of hauling the big guns up and down the steep Pennsylvania hills slowed the army considerably.

Washington's Guessing Game

At about 9:45, Knyphausen began his great diversion. As he approached Chadds Ford,

General Nathanael Greene was ordered to protect Chadds Ford, the likeliest point of British attack along Brandywine Creek.

an American advance force under General Maxwell met Knyphausen on the southwest side of the river. Riddling the exposed British troops with musket fire from sheltered positions, Maxwell's men delayed the advance for an hour and a half. After inflicting three hundred casualties with little loss, they scuttled back across the river to the

The Commander in Chief

Congress's choice of George Washington as commander of the Continental army in 1775 proved to be a wiser choice than even his supporters at that time realized. Washington was born in 1732 to a prosperous landowner from a well-established Virginia family; Washington's father had accumulated ten thousand acres by the time of his death in 1743. Although he had little formal schooling, Washington was adept at mathematics and at the age of sixteen began working as a surveyor. In addition to his inherited lands, he purchased several thousand acres on his own, then became one of the wealthiest men in America when he married widow Martha Custis in 1758.

Washington's military experience prior to the Revolution was undistinguished. As a major in the French and Indian War, Washington led an expedition that was surrounded by the French and forced to surrender in 1754. Promoted to colonel, he fought bravely in the disastrous defeat of General Braddock's army the following year. Since that time, he had spent most of his life managing a plantation and dabbling in politics.

When the Continental Congress sought an overall commander for its army, it had little from which to choose. Washington's experience in the French and Indian War, together with his impressive stature and manner and his status as a gentleman, placed him in the running. But in the end, the job went to him primarily because New Englander John Adams wanted a Virginian to command the army in order to broaden support for the war in the South.

Washington had mixed feelings about taking the command. Pessimistic about the colonies' chances in such a war, he worried that he was setting himself up for failure. Even if he was not hung as a traitor, people would blame him for the war's failure and his reputation would be ruined. On the other hand, he felt that honor required him to answer his country's call. In the end, he accepted the position with resignation. "As it has been a kind of destiny that has thrown me upon this service, I shall hope that my undertaking it is designed to some good purpose," he wrote in a letter quoted by Robert Middlekauff in *The Glorious Cause: The American Revolution, 1763–1789.*

Throughout the war, Washington's critics constantly criticized him. At one point a group of influential politicians worked hard to replace him with Horatio Gates, but Washington's determination and the loyalty of his officers and troops kept him in command. Given Gates's subsequent performance at Camden, South Carolina, such a move would have greatly hurt the colonial cause. Historians credit Washington not only with keeping his army together and using it effectively on occasion but with helping to build support for the young nation by unfailingly treating the Continental Congress with utmost respect.

American lines. Knyphausen then made a great show of marching troops around in plain sight to make the Americans think that Howe's entire army was before them and preparing a frontal assault.

In the meantime, Washington began to get conflicting reports about the British flanking maneuver. At about 11 A.M., when word reached him that British troops had been seen marching north, he assigned two brigades under Colonel Theodrick Bland to the extreme right wing of the army in case Howe attacked from that side. Another message from spies confirmed that at least five thousand British had been seen heading north.

The news that Howe had divided his army presented Washington with a golden opportunity. He could beat Howe to the punch and overwhelm Knyphausen's force at Chadds Ford before Cornwallis could get back into the picture. Washington ordered a full-scale attack on Knyphausen, but just as it was beginning, he got a strongly worded message from Sullivan's division that the locals reported no British moving north. Washington concluded that the initial reports had been false information sent out by some of the many Loyalists in the area. The supposed flanking march was just a decoy to draw him into the huge blunder of leaving his entrenched position to attack the huge British force at Chadds Ford. Washington not only called off that attack, but recalled Bland's two brigades from the north.

But a patriotic farmer named Thomas Cheyney had seen the massive British crossing with his own eyes. He rode hard to the American headquarters and demanded to talk to Washington personally. When he heard Cheyney's story, Washington did not know what to think. For all he knew, Cheyney was a double agent sent to feed him false information.

While Washington was trying to sift the truth out of conflicting reports, at about 1:15 Cornwallis's army completed its river crossing and began bearing down on the Americans from the northwest. Washington's confusion at this point was crucial because the British then had to march through a narrow gorge, so ideal for defense that a small group of Americans could

have held them bottled up almost indefinitely.

It was not until two o'clock when further reports came in that Washington was finally convinced that Howe had again successfully flanked him. He realized now that his army was caught badly out of position, just as it had been at Long Island. Cornwallis

Patriotic farmer Thomas Cheyney brings news to Washington of the British crossing of Brandywine Creek at Jeffries Ford.

had seized the high ground of Osbourne's Hill behind the American right flank before his enemy knew he was there.

Howe's Hesitation

Now, the main flaw in Howe's otherwise solid leadership showed itself. Historian Craig Symonds observes, "Typically, however, Howe hesitated before launching the blow that might have destroyed Washington's army."[42] Throughout the war, in fact, Howe had displayed a lack of urgency in finishing off his opponent. Previously, his lack of a killer instinct had let Washington off the ropes after the Americans' humiliating disasters in New York. Some military analysts suggest that he was overly cautious by nature; some believe he made the mistake of repeatedly underestimating his opponent. Others speculate that Howe, who had been outspokenly sympathetic to the American cause before the war, simply lacked the heart to pursue victory with the needed passion.

Whatever the reason, Howe decided that, after marching fourteen miles in the heat to outflank the Americans, Cornwallis's men deserved to rest and eat before he sent them into action. The delay gave away some of the advantage for which they had marched so long and gave Sullivan a chance to pivot his division nearly ninety degrees to face the attack.

American Blunders

Howe's delay played so well into the American hands that, had their leaders executed the redeployment maneuvers skillfully, their army might have been able to recover and negate Howe's advantage. But Sullivan marched some of his troops too far to the north and left a gap in his line of defense.

At around four o'clock that afternoon, Cornwallis finally received the order to launch his attack. He sent two British divisions and one Hessian division into battle, split into eight sections. The fighting along what came to be known as Battle Hill was perhaps the fiercest sustained battle of the entire war. The finest troops in the British army charged with steel discipline all along the line. They poured through the gap in Sullivan's line and smashed through all resistance. Sullivan's men retreated and reformed their lines about eight hundred yards to the rear.

At this point, another American leader, the French general Prudhomme de Borre, made an unforgivable blunder. When Sullivan ordered de Borre's men to fill in the gap caused by his misalignment, de Borre haughtily refused. In an incredible display of letting ego get in the way of duty, he insisted on being given the position of honor in the army, which in his mind was at the extreme flank. Therefore, de Borre marched his men even farther to the north and left the gap for the British to exploit.

Their leadership blunders, combined with the fact that they were outnumbered more than two to one, put the Americans on the right in a desperate position. Wielding their bayonets with lethal efficiency, the British repeatedly broke through the Amer-

Spies

Both sides relied heavily on spies to keep them posted as to their enemy's movements. The problem was, with Loyalists and Patriots living side by side and in many cases keeping their preferences hidden, it was difficult to know who was spying for whom. Historians R. Ernest Dupuy and Trevor N. Dupuy in *An Outline History of the American Revolution* write, "New Jersey was a land of spies, most of them double agents, hundreds of them moving freely in and out of the American and British camps." It was a dangerous game because, while the regular armies generally treated prisoners with civility, spies were routinely executed. A spy was identified as anyone operating secretly behind enemy lines, wearing a disguise, or carrying documents that proved he was a spy.

The two most famous spies of the war were Nathan Hale and John André. Hale was a teacher from Connecticut who served as a spy for Washington during the New York campaigns. Captured on Long Island on September 21, he was hung by the British on September 22, 1776. His oft-quoted final words, as quoted in *An Outline History of the American Revolution*, "I only regret that I have but one life to lose for my country," inspired patriotic fervor throughout the colonies.

André was a British officer who made a dangerous rendezvous with Benedict Arnold in September 1780 as part of Arnold's scheme to betray West Point. André secretly departed from the British ship *Vulture*, anchored in the Hudson River, to meet with Arnold at the fort. But before he could return to the ship, American gunfire had forced it to retreat downstream.

As he rode south to catch up with it, André still believed he was in no danger. He carried written orders from Arnold authorizing him to travel where he wished through American lines. But as he approached a British outpost, he made the fatal error of assuming he had reached safety. When he was stopped on the road by three men, he misjudged where American control ended and British control began, and he identified himself as a British officer.

The men, however, were Patriots. Searching André, they discovered plans for the betrayal of West Point in his boot.

Like Hale, André was condemned to die, which he did with equal grace. His last words, quoted in Cumming and Rankin's *The Fate of a Nation,* were: "I pray you bear me witness that I meet my fate like a brave man."

American spy Nathan Hale awaits his execution by the British.

ican defensive lines on the slopes above the Brandywine. Sullivan frantically tried to rally his troops, but they lacked the professional discipline of their enemies. As Sullivan later reported, "No sooner did I form one party than that which I had formed would run off."[43]

Where the Americans did manage to reform their defensive lines, the British met with determined resistance. In the words of a British captain, "The fire of Musketry all this time was as Incessant and Tremendous; as ever had been Remembered."[44]

The Fighting at Chadds Ford

During the early stages of the fight, Washington continued to fear that the movement on his flank was just a diversion and that the main attack would come from Knyphausen at Chadds Ford. But by five o'clock, the thunder of Cornwallis's cannons and the relative lack of activity from Knyphausen finally convinced him that his main peril was on the right. He found a

American militia repel a British attack during the Battle of Brandywine.

farmer who knew the land well and got him to rush Washington and two of Greene's divisions to Sullivan's defense.

In the meantime, back at Chadds Ford, Knyphausen's army had finally joined in the attack, beginning with a tremendous artillery barrage. With Greene's divisions having been committed to support Sullivan, there was now no support for the soldiers of General Anthony Wayne in their defense of the ford. The success of the battle depended upon their ability to stop Knyphausen by themselves.

In fact, they were handling that responsibility well when a bizarre bit of misfortune struck. The far right unit of Cornwallis's assault had gotten lost in the thick woods and hills and had blundered past Sullivan's division without ever seeing them. This error undoubtedly allowed Sullivan's men to hold out longer than they otherwise would have, but the British emerged from the woods to find themselves in the rear of Wayne's force. Caught in crossfire, Wayne had no choice but to pull men off the front line to deal with this new attack. Further weakened by this, the defensive line facing Knyphausen gave way after a bitter fight. Wayne's men had to retreat so quickly that they left behind their artillery and many other supplies.

Courageous American Stands

Despite their huge disadvantage caused by Howe's flanking maneuver, the Americans avoided annihilation thanks to a series of courageous acts by their troops. The men

Philadelphia

Washington felt an obligation to defend Philadelphia because of its symbolic value to the colonies. The city, founded by Quaker William Penn, had grown to forty thousand people, nearly twice the size of the second-largest American city, New York. Because of its relatively central location, it had been selected as the meeting place of the Continental Congress. The city had also become one of the nation's leading manufacturing centers, especially in the production of weapons, gunpowder, and other supplies necessary to the war effort. Although the colonies had no national capitol, Philadelphia's size and status made it the next best thing, and Washington, to whom honor was of utmost importance, felt that its loss would be a blow to the nation's pride.

on Sullivan's extreme right held out determinedly. A British officer reported: "By six o'clock our left wing still had not been able to advance. Here the rebels fought very bravely and did not retreat until they heard in their rear General Knyphausen's fire coming near."[45] Their brave stand kept the British from surrounding the Americans and forcing the surrender of Washington's entire army.

Greene's divisions won praise for their remarkable exhibition of speed and endurance in covering the hilly, four-mile distance to Sullivan's aid in forty-five minutes. They arrived too late to stem the British advance, but they did save Sullivan's division from disaster. As the men fighting on the front lines finally fell into headlong retreat, Greene's men opened up their lines to let them pass through and then closed to fight off the British advance. They nearly paid a high price for their bravery. Unaware that Wayne's force had been driven back and that they were the only Americans still fighting, they found themselves attacked on three sides by Cornwallis from the north and west

Polish general Casimir Pulaski led a cavalry charge that complicated the British advance at Brandywine and helped the American army avoid capture.

and by Knyphausen from the south. They managed to fall back in reasonably good order given the circumstances, which kept the road to Philadelphia open for the rest of the army to flee. Polish general Casimir Pulaski led a particularly effective cavalry charge that temporarily stopped the British in their tracks. One final American foray, as darkness began to settle on the field, inflicted heavy casualties on the British.

British Victory, American Survival

Despite these acts of heroism, however, the American army was still extremely vulnerable. Sullivan's division had been severely battered, and Wayne's men had been forced to retreat in such haste that most of the army was scattered in confusion along the road for at least twelve miles. Once again, they benefited from Howe's lack of aggression. The last American counterattack had been fierce enough to give Howe second thoughts about continuing the fight. Again concerned about the condition of his men who had fought for more than three hours after having marched nearly as long, he decided to content himself with having driven the Americans from the battlefield. The British halted at the Brandywine for several days to refresh themselves before continuing their advance on Philadelphia.

The Battle of Brandywine was unquestionably a British victory. Estimates of the casualties in the battle vary considerably, but Howe reported 90 of his men killed, 488 wounded, and 6 missing. The Americans left the field in such confusion that their figures

The Paoli Massacre

Following the Battle of Brandywine, Washington retreated to the west, leaving General "Mad Anthony" Wayne and fifteen hundred men lurking in the woods near Paoli, Pennsylvania, to cause trouble for Howe. Wayne wrote to Washington that he was convinced the British had no knowledge of his presence. Loyalist spies in the area, however, had detected the American troops and had informed the British.

On the night of September 20, 1777, five thousand British troops under Major General Charles Grey crept up on Wayne's men. They had removed the flint from their muskets so that there could be no accidental firings to alert the enemy of their presence, and they relied totally on bayonets and swords. At one o'clock in the morning, they crashed through Wayne's pickets and descended on his unprepared camp.

A British officer described the scene, as quoted by Cumming and Rankin in *The Fate of a Nation:* "The enemy were completely surprised, some with arms, others without, running in all directions in the greatest confusion. The light infantry bayoneted every man they came up with. The camp was immediately set on fire, and this, and the cries of the wounded, formed altogether one of the most dreadful scenes I ever beheld."

The extent of the slaughter that came to be known among Americans as the Paoli Massacre varies depending on the source. Estimates of the losses suffered by the Americans range from 53 to 421 killed, with British losses pegged at anywhere from 4 to 20 killed. Either way, the conflict was dreadfully one-sided. The trauma of the night and the way in which it was administered, however, helped bond Wayne's men. They constantly sought a chance to avenge themselves, and for the rest of the war British troops were extremely wary of confronting Wayne's division.

are unknown but are believed to have been nearly twice that of the British. More importantly, Howe again outmaneuvered Washington and drove him from the strongest defensive position available to him in protecting Philadelphia. However, Howe once again failed to follow up on his success and left Washington, although weakened, free to fight another day.

American Leaders' Performance at Brandywine

Washington was heavily criticized at the time, and has been since, for falling victim to the same flanking maneuver that Howe had pulled on him in New York. On the other hand, it was not a case of Washington's failing to learn his lesson and being outwitted again. The general was well aware of the possibility that Howe would try a flanking movement to his right and had taken precautions to prevent it from happening. When he neglected his right wing, it was only on the basis of false scouting reports that told him that there were no fords in the vicinity upstream and that the British were not marching in that direction. Once Washington received solid information on Cornwallis's whereabouts, he had moved decisively to counter his foe. The failure of those moves rests primarily with Sullivan and, especially, de Borre. In fact, both were removed from their commands following the battle. If Washington is to be criticized for his performance at Brandywine, it is for the ineptness of his scouting system.

Historians have speculated as to what would have happened had Washington carried through with his initial order to attack Knyphausen once he suspected that Howe had divided his army. Some believe that, had he attacked with his entire army, he could have overwhelmed Knyphausen before Cornwallis completed his march and then would have been able to deal separately with Cornwallis. But a more common belief is that of W. J. Wood: "In retrospect it was probably fortunate that the attack was canceled."[46] Washington had a strong defensive position at Brandywine, not a strong offensive position, and he would have given that up had he tried to cross the river against Knyphausen. With seven thousand men and a strong battery of artillery, Knyphausen likely could have inflicted heavy losses on the Americans and held them off until Cornwallis arrived from the rear. Whether the American army could have escaped from that situation is doubtful.

Long-Term Results of Brandywine

Howe's timidity in letting Washington go very nearly cost him dearly a few weeks later, on October 4, when Washington made one last attack to blunt the British advance on

In this contemporary reenactment, riflemen form a defensive line against a British advance.

Philadelphia. This time it was Washington who moved his army with the greater skill and surprised Howe's army at a small town near Philadelphia known as Germantown. The furious American charge rocked the superior British army on its heels and came surprisingly close to succeeding before it was doomed by yet another example of inept American leadership. General Adam Stephen had been ordered to cover the left flank of Wayne's army, which was carrying the brunt of the attack. Stephen, however, who was reportedly drunk, misplaced his men and brought them straight into Wayne's rear. They then compounded their mistake by opening fire in the belief that Wayne was the enemy. Believing themselves surrounded, Wayne's men halted their successful attack and turned to fight the troops at their back. In the confusion, the British regrouped and organized an effective counterattack that threw back the Americans.

With that defeat, which cost the Americans 673 killed and wounded and 400 captured, compared to 521 casualties for the British, the Americans had to abandon their effort to protect Philadelphia. The British occupied the city on September 26, 1777. The immediate result, then, of Washington's defeat at Brandywine was that it opened the door to the British conquest of America's most important city.

On the other hand, Howe's inability to defeat Washington allowed the revolution to continue. As Washington well knew, the longer his army stayed in the field, the costlier the war would be to Great Britain and the greater the pressure on the British to give up and go home. Washington retreated from Philadelphia to Valley Forge where, although his army suffered terrible deprivations over the winter, he kept it intact. It emerged as a significant fighting force in the spring of 1778, which contributed to the British rethinking their war strategy. Following the Battle of Monmouth, which the armies fought to a draw in June 1778, they shifted their emphasis from conquering the North and concentrated on strengthening their grip on the South.

Chapter 6

Kings Mountain

A lthough the American Revolution is often depicted as a war between the armies of the American colonists and the British Empire, neither the Continental army nor the British army was present at one of the most important battles of the war. Kings Mountain was the site of a fight between a well-organized group of Americans loyal to the British and a loosely organized collection of frontiersmen who opposed them.

New Strategy for the British

Despite Howe's victories at Brandywine and Germantown and the occupation of both New York City and Philadelphia, the British government was not pleased with the progress of the war in 1779. Neither Howe nor the man who succeeded him as overall commander that year, General Henry Clinton, were able to inflict a crippling defeat on Washington's army. Because of this, the war dragged on, and it was costing the British government far more than it thought it could afford.

In late 1779, therefore, the British undertook to relieve the financial burden with a change in strategy. Rather than having British troops do all the fighting, they would

British general Henry Clinton had many military successes in the Revolutionary War, but he was unable to deal a crippling blow to Washington's army.

shift more of the burden to American Loyalists. Believing that the South was largely unsympathetic to independence, they targeted this region first. Their strategy was to provide weapons and leadership to the Loyalists in South Carolina and Georgia. Once these areas were secured, they would sweep northward, collecting Loyalists and intimidating Patriots as they went, until they joined with Clinton's main regular army in New York.

Some of the British officers in the field, including General Clinton, had doubts about the plan. Why trust the war to an army of Loyalists who, in their opinion, could never match the fighting skill of the professional British army? They also suspected that, even in the South, most Americans were not interested in fighting for either side but just wanted to be left alone.

Nevertheless, Clinton followed orders and launched the new strategy by sailing with a large army of British regulars and Northern Loyalists to South Carolina. He had little trouble outmaneuvering the American opposition, led by Benjamin Lincoln. On May 12, 1780, he captured the key coastal city of Charleston, thereby laying the South open to invasion. Clinton then returned to his troops in New York to continue his standoff with Washington, leaving General Cornwallis in charge of operations.

A Savage Civil War: Patriots Versus Loyalists

The British set about putting the new strategy into action—recruiting and persuading

Clinton outmaneuvered Benjamin Lincoln (pictured) in South Carolina, opening the South to invasion.

the citizens to renounce the rebel cause and take up arms for the king. Some of them went about this humanely. Among those was Major Patrick Ferguson, an enterprising Scottish officer who was convinced he could train Loyalists to be a disciplined and effective fighting force. In 1779, he had taken command of a group of three hundred Loyalists from New York and New Jersey and

On the other hand, some British officers relied on cruelty and intimidation to achieve their ends. Foremost among these was Lieutenant Colonel Banastre Tarleton. As he toured South Carolina, Tarleton gave American men the choice of serving in the Loyalist army or having their crops and houses burned. On May 29, 1780, he earned the lasting hatred of Patriots at the Battle of Waxhaws. On that occasion, his troops slaughtered a large group of American militia who were attempting to surrender. More than 100 Americans died at Waxhaws and only 53 of the 203 taken captive escaped without wounds. Tarleton's behavior earned him the nickname Bloody Ban, and the act of killing unarmed, defenseless enemies became known as Tarleton's Quarter.

The terror imposed by men such as Tarleton triggered violent retaliation. Before long, the formerly complacent South had split into bitterly divided camps. In the Carolinas and Georgia, the war of independence dissolved into a civil war in which each side tried to annihilate the other. At one point, American general Nathanael Greene reported, "The Whigs and Tories persecute each other with little less than Savage fury. There is nothing but murders and devastations in every quarter."[48]

British Advance

The Continental Congress attempted to put a national army in the field under General

Colonel Banastre Tarleton was hated by Patriots for the atrocities he committed against captured American soldiers.

had brought them south with Clinton's force. He recruited a large number of Loyalists, many of whom were not particularly respected members of society. In the words of a contemporary, "His camp became at once the rendezvous of the desperate, the idle, and vindictive, as well as zealous Loyalist youth."[47] Yet Ferguson managed to mold them into a well-disciplined fighting force and was widely admired by both his troops and civilians.

Gates to defend the South. But on August 16, 1780, Cornwallis soundly defeated Gates at Camden, South Carolina, leaving the American army shattered. The British commander's master strategy was proceeding flawlessly. Georgia was under British control and Patriot resistance in South Carolina was limited to hit-and-run raiders such as Francis the "Swamp Fox" Marion, who could strike a British target quickly and disappear into the wilderness before they were caught. Cornwallis then turned north to continue with the next phase of the strategy.

While the raids of people like Marion posed no threat to Cornwallis, they were ir-ritating. Cornwallis felt that in order to encourage Loyalists to continue joining his cause, he had to control the destruction and terror inflicted on isolated Loyalists. As he began his march to North Carolina that fall, he dispatched orders to Ferguson, who was encamped at Fort Ninety-Six, South Carolina. Ferguson was to march north with his one thousand Loyalist troops to protect Cornwallis's left flank from rebel raids, to quash resistance among the Patriots and recruit Loyalists along the way.

At the Battle of Camden, the British soundly defeated the rebels, shattering the American army.

Ferguson Riles the
Over Mountain Men

In late September, Ferguson approached the North Carolina–South Carolina border about seventy miles west of Charlotte, to which Cornwallis was advancing with the main army. While he knew that the people of the western Carolinas tended to favor the Patriot cause, Ferguson was unaware of how deeply those feelings ran, particularly after

Hit-and-run raiders like Francis Marion led many raids on British targets in South Carolina.

reports of atrocities committed by men like Tarleton had circulated. Upon learning that one of his soldiers was a relative of Isaac Shelby, a local rebel leader, Ferguson had the man send a message to his kinsman warning the rebels to stop their hostile activities. Uncharacteristically, Ferguson employed some of Tarleton's intimidation tactics. He threatened to march his army over the mountains to deal with the rebels, hang their leaders, and "lay the country waste with fire and sword." [49]

Even those among the western settlers who were inclined to mind their own business and stay out of the war reacted with cold fury. Word spread among them that this arrogant enemy needed to be taught a lesson. On September 25, a group of some eight hundred of the fiercest, wildest men in the land began to assemble for just that purpose. These men, nicknamed the Over Mountain Men, did not pretend to be an army. To the contrary, they had nothing but contempt for the precise discipline of the enemy's marches and formations. One contemporary observer gave a detailed description of them: "On their heads they wore caps of coonskin or minkskin with the tails hanging down, or else felt hats on which was thrust a Buck's tail or a sprig of evergreen. Every man carried a small bore rifle, a tomahawk, and a scalping knife. A very few of the men had swords and there was not a bayonet or tent in the whole army." [50] A few days later, they were joined by another 550 men. This was still 1,000 fewer than Ferguson was believed to have under his command, but the possibility of being outnumbered did not faze them in the least. On two occasions, the leaders gathered the men and offered any who wished the chance to turn back. Not a man accepted the offer.

Most of the Over Mountain Men were mounted on horseback, and they rode toward Ferguson's position with a smoldering intensity. Their intention was not to defeat the Loyalist army or to drive them off, but to annihilate them. Upon hearing a rumor that Ferguson was running away to the east to join Cornwallis, the leaders made a quick decision. The fastest seven hundred riders would take off with all speed to catch the enemy before they could escape. The rest would follow and join the fight as soon as they were able.

Ferguson Digs In at Kings Mountain

Meanwhile, Ferguson's spies had reported to him the advance of the Over Mountain Men. In response, he did move closer to Cornwallis, as his enemies feared he would. But rather than join the main force, he stopped about 30 miles away at a spur of the Blue Ridge Mountains known as Kings Mountain. It was hardly a mountain; in fact, it rose only 60 feet above the surrounding land before it flattened into a small plateau 600 feet long and from 70 to 120 feet wide. But the heavily forested slopes were steep, and one side was sheer rock. A commonly held principle of war was that the advantage went to the army with the high ground, and Ferguson decided that the commanding

Washington's Close Call

British major Patrick Ferguson was the key figure in the third of Washington's close brushes with death or capture. On September 8, 1777, Washington and another officer rode out into the hills to study the land between the British forces and Chadds Ford, which Washington planned to defend. They rode directly into the sights of four British sharpshooters, including Ferguson, concealed in the brush. Ferguson had no idea who the men were, but instead of shooting them, Ferguson tried to capture them. He ordered Washington's companion, who was closer, to surrender. But the man shouted a warning to Washington, who calmly turned and galloped away with his companion.

While Washington was fleeing, Ferguson had him in his sights and could easily have shot him but declined to pull the trigger. Even when he later learned who the horseman was, Ferguson never regretted his decision. As reported by Mark Mayo Boatner III in *Encyclopedia of the American Revolution*, Ferguson later remarked, "It was not pleasant to fire at the back of an unoffending individual who was acquitting himself very coolly of his duty, so I let him alone."

view and the difficulty an attacking force would have scaling the slopes made Kings Mountain an ideal defensive position. He wrote to Cornwallis, "I have taken a post [position] where I do not think I can be forced." Furthermore, continuing his ill-advised cockiness, he claimed that he could defend it against "God Almighty and all the rebels of hell."[51]

Ferguson's bristling confidence, however, did not prevent him from requesting, in almost the same breath, reinforcements of three hundred men from Cornwallis.

The trees on the slopes of Kings Mountain provide cover for the Americans.

Those reinforcements did not arrive; Cornwallis could only assume from the rest of Ferguson's remarks that they were not desperately needed.

While Ferguson was preparing his defenses, the Over Mountain Men traveled all through the night and all the next morning to meet him. At shortly after noon on Saturday, October 7, they arrived at Kings Mountain. So eager were they for the fight that they declined to wait for their slower comrades before beginning the battle. Since they had no officers and were not differentiated by rank, they chose their leader by vote. William Campbell, who won the honor, was a fiery man with little interest in battle tactics. Given the temperament of his men, any organized plan would probably have been useless anyway. But Campbell simply told the men to "shout like hell and fight like devils."[52] Then they dispersed around the sides of the mountain to do their damage. At three o'clock, the assault began.

Potential Death Trap

The fighting had scarcely begun when Ferguson discovered that the rules of war did not necessarily apply when fighting Americans. His supposedly strong defensive position turned out to be a death trap. Although he had been correct in thinking that the heights gave him an advantage and that the attackers would be exposed to fire as they climbed the steep, rocky slopes, he had failed to realize that his men would have to stand up to fire at the enemy and would be exposed to fire themselves in the process. The three heavily forested other sides presented an even greater problem for the defenders. Against a traditional foe attacking in formation, the thick woods would have helped the defenders by hindering the enemy's advance. But the Over Mountain Men had no use for formations. As they crept up the slopes individually, the trees offered shelter. Slowly, they advanced up the hill, firing from cover. Some of them climbed into the trees, from which they had a clear view of the British defenders. While they knew nothing of bayonet attacks and battle tactics, the Over Mountain Men were skilled hunters. They could pick off a target at far greater distances and with far greater accuracy than the Loyalist defenders could.

Camden and the Fall of Horatio Gates

Horatio Gates was not a favorite of many of his fellow American generals. Washington, Arnold, Morgan, and Greene, among others, all had reason to dislike or mistrust him. But Gates happened to be the man in charge at the Americans' greatest triumph of the war, Saratoga. This, and the fact that he had friends in high political places, gained him a reputation far greater than his ability. Against Washington's wishes, Congress assigned Gates the task of defending the South against Cornwallis's offensive in the summer of 1780.

Gates decided to seize the offensive. Without making provision for adequate supplies, he marched his army of some four thousand men to Camden, South Carolina, where he hoped to defeat a small British force. Cornwallis, learning of Gates's actions, moved north with one thousand men to double the size of the British garrison to twenty-two hundred. The two armies met on August 16, five miles north of Camden.

Although Gates had the larger army, he made the mistake of putting all his militia on the left and seasoned Continental soldiers on the right. The British overwhelmed the militia, many of whom were so panicked that they ran off without firing a shot. With them rode General Gates, who rode all the way to Charlotte, while his second in command, General Baron de Kalb, died in a valiant attempt to hold his lines in the face of disaster. With their left unsupported, the Continentals were caught in a vise between two British forces and mauled.

The Americans suffered an estimated six hundred fatalities and one thousand men captured, which all but destroyed the Continental army in the South, which now consisted of eight hundred starving, leaderless soldiers. British casualties were recorded as only 79 killed and 245 wounded. Gates's stunning flight from the battlefield cost him his command and reputation. He was soon replaced by Nathanael Greene. Among the sarcastic comments directed at his actions was that of future secretary of the treasury, Alexander Hamilton. In *An Outline History of the American Revolution*, R. Ernest Dupuy and Trevor N. Dupuy quote him as writing, "One hundred and eighty miles in three days and a half! It does admirable credit to the activity of a man at this time of life."

The most serious defect of Ferguson's Kings Mountain defense, however, was that he had left himself no line of retreat. If he was unable to fight off the attack, his men would have no choice but to surrender or go down fighting. Given the bitterness that existed between the Loyalists and the Patriots, surrendering promised to be a most unattractive option.

Bayonet Charges Versus Sniper Fire

Ferguson, however, was an able commander, and he had trained his troops well. Using signals in the form of blasts from a silver whistle to direct his men in the din of battle, he formed a bayonet charge that drove the attackers from one of the slopes. But while he was doing so, another group crept up another slope, laying down deadly fire as they advanced. Ferguson formed a second line of troops who successfully drove the enemy off the slopes with their bayonets.

The attackers, though, were all over the slopes, joined by some of the slower riders who had reached Kings Mountain in time to join the fight. Ferguson tried to shift his troops to meet one challenge and then reform to meet another. Ferguson's men were reduced to using bayonets while the enemy used their rifles with devastating results. Before long, the Patriots were swarming near the summit and, firing from cover, had clear shots at the Loyalists.

The Loyalists held out valiantly as long as Ferguson tirelessly directed them. But, unlike the British, who considered the targeting of officers uncivilized, the Patriots had no qualms about aiming for their enemy's leaders. Easily recognized by his whistle, Ferguson came under a hail of rifle fire. About an hour into the battle, he fell from his horse, fatally wounded by perhaps a dozen shots. His second in command immediately raised a white flag to surrender. The surrender did not immediately end the violence, however. A combination of communication difficulties among the fighters scattered over the slopes and lingering bitterness over both Ferguson's threats and the memory of Tarleton's Quarter led to some of the Loyalists being wounded or killed after they had laid down their weapons. Even after the Patriot leaders gained control of the situation and stopped the fighting, abuse of the vanquished continued. Many of the prisoners were beaten, some even killed, as they were marched away from Kings Mountain to be delivered to Continental authorities. And in retaliation for the recent British execution of forty-one Patriots as traitors to the crown, the Patriots then hanged two Loyalist officers.

The battle proved to be yet another of the stunningly one-sided contests that characterized the American Revolution. Loyalist losses were 225 dead, 163 wounded, and 716 taken prisoner. The cost to the Patriots was only 28 killed and 68 wounded.

Exactly who should be held responsible for the Loyalist defeat is a matter of debate. While Ferguson committed a major blunder in putting his army in a corner, Cornwallis shares some of the blame for allowing Ferguson to operate in isolation. The superior numbers and training of the British and Loyalist armies in the region was wasted when Cornwallis's army was too far from the battlefield to offer assistance.

Significance of Kings Mountain

Many historians consider the Battle of Kings Mountain to have been even more impor-

tant to the American cause than the triumph at Saratoga. Thomas Jefferson later wrote of it: "That glorious victory was the joyful annunciation of that turn in the tide of success which terminated the Revolutionary War."[53]

Such statements reflect the fact that the Patriot cause, despite Washington's

General Ferguson falls from his horse as he is fatally wounded by American rifle fire.

Charleston: America's Most Devastating Loss of the War

The British had made two attempts to capture the port city of Charleston, South Carolina, early in the war, once by land and once by sea. Both attempts failed. Now with the British shifting their focus to the South, the capture of Charleston took on renewed importance. On December 26, 1779, General Clinton left fifteen thousand men under General Knyphausen to hold New York while he sailed with eighty-five hundred troops and fourteen warships to the South. Storms made the voyage difficult, and it was not until February 11 that the army finally disembarked thirty miles south of Charleston.

The Americans entrusted defense of the city to twenty-six hundred Continentals and nearly three thousand militia. Having learned from their previous failures, the British methodically set about to surround the city. On March 6, Clinton struck from the south, capturing Fort Johnson. With his forces boosted to ten thousand men, he crossed the Ashley River and constructed trenches, sealing off the city from the south. On April 8, a British fleet sailed past Fort Moultrie, which was supposed to protect the city from the ocean side. Finally, on April 14, Tarleton drove off the American forces by the Cooper River and blocked any exit to the north.

Having surrounded the city, Clinton began closing in. By April 19, he had moved his troops to within two hundred yards of Charleston's west side and prepared his heavy artillery to level the city. At that point, General Benjamin Lincoln's only hope of saving his Continental army was a breakout attempt. But the city government let him know that they considered such an action a cowardly abandonment of the city and persuaded him to stay. On May 9, Clinton turned his cannons on the city and the devastation so grieved the city leaders that now they asked Lincoln to surrender so the city could be spared such destruction. Seeing that any hopes of escaping had long passed, Lincoln agreed. On May 12, he surrendered 5,500 American troops as well as the city. It was by far the largest American loss of troops in the war.

The fall of Charleston launched the British offensive in the South. It intimidated Patriots into hiding and emboldened Loyalists, who soon were able to gain almost total control of most of South Carolina as well as Georgia.

valiant efforts to hold his army together, was in disarray prior to Kings Mountain. The Patriots had gone more than two years without a single military success, and the British appeared to have found a strategy that was working. In the South, particularly, the Patriots had suffered a series of devastating defeats: the surrender of Charleston, the disaster at Camden, and Tarleton's brutal repression. Much of the countryside was being terrorized and intimidated into submission. Georgia was in complete control of the British, opposition in South Carolina had been scattered, and North Carolina and Virginia appeared certain to fall next.

Most of the Over Mountain Men who fought at Kings Mountain did not stay to become part of the Continental army. Theirs was primarily a personal, passionate interest in defending their homes and families from a direct threat by Ferguson. Having destroyed that threat and the man who made it, they returned to their homes in the west. But with their stunning victory at Kings Mountain, the Over Mountain Men awakened a new spirit of optimism in the rebel cause in the South.

On a more practical level, by wiping out Ferguson's Loyalists, they destroyed the entire left wing of Cornwallis's army. Unwilling to leave himself exposed to the ravages of the unpredictable Patriot militia, Cornwallis had to halt his march into North Carolina, retreat, and reform. The momentum created by the new strategy had been disrupted. The Patriots used this period of regrouping to strengthen their own military situation so that when the British moved again, they would be ready.

Chapter 7

Cowpens

ven though the Over Mountain Men's destruction of Ferguson's army at Kings Mountain provided some crucial breathing room, the Continental army in the South was in bad shape at the end of 1780. Nathanael Greene, who had replaced Gates as commander, was a good organizer but needed time to rebuild the shattered army. His total force, as of December, was no larger than fifteen hundred poorly supplied men.

Realizing that his army was not strong enough to mount a direct challenge to Cornwallis, Greene looked for ways to continue harassing the enemy while he worked at building his strength. In mid-December, he sent six hundred men under the direction of Daniel Morgan to western South Carolina with orders to protect Patriots and annoy Loyalists in the area.

A letter that Greene wrote later in the campaign shows the caution that he urged upon the fearless Morgan. "I do not wish you should come to action unless you have a manifest superiority, and a moral certainty of succeeding. Put nothing to the hazard. A retreat may be disagreeable, but not disgraceful. . . . It is not our business to risk too much. Our affairs are in too critical a situation."[54]

A Trap for Daniel Morgan

Upon learning from his spies that Greene had split his army, Cornwallis was pleasantly stunned. Military leaders seldom risked dividing their forces in the face of a superior enemy, and Greene had done just that. Cornwallis calculated that if he acted quickly, he could trap Morgan's small force and easily capture or destroy it. He had just the officer for carrying out such an aggressive campaign—Banastre Tarleton.

By this time, Tarleton had developed a reputation for brilliant and efficient—as well as ruthless—leadership. His dreaded Legion had ridden 105 miles in fifty-four hours to chase down the fleeing Patriot band at Waxhaws. Then, despite being outnumbered, he had thrown his troops into the fray with such skill and fury that they had annihilated their foe. In August, he had achieved similar success against the popular rebel leader Thomas Sumter. Again, Tarleton's Legion had made a remarkable ride to catch the Patriots, attacked with a much smaller force than the enemy, and overwhelmed them. Since then, Tarleton had spent much of his time roaming through the South Carolina countryside, burning the houses and crops of Patriots and killing their livestock.

Cornwallis provided Tarleton with two regiments of infantry in addition to his mounted Legion. This gave Tarleton eleven hundred men, the largest force he had ever commanded, and he was determined to use his strength to the fullest. On January 6, 1781, he started after Morgan at his usual exhausting pace. Meanwhile, Cornwallis began marching his main army northwest to cut off any possibility of Morgan getting help from Greene.

The Trap Closes

Morgan's men at this time were in a difficult position, due to their leader's refusal to bring supply wagons. "Wagons would be an impediment whether we attempt to annoy the enemy or provide for our own safety,"[55] he had said. Although this decision allowed his army to move quickly, it forced them constantly to send out foraging parties in search of food. When his capable spy network alerted him that Tarleton was in hot pursuit, he wondered how he could spare soldiers for food gathering. Concerned that he

would not be able to feed his army for long under these conditions, he asked Greene's permission either to retreat into Georgia or to rejoin Greene. Greene responded that Morgan was to stay in South Carolina. In that

In 1780 Daniel Morgan lead a force into South Carolina to protect Patriots in the area.

case, Morgan asked, would Greene help him out by making some move to draw the British attention away from him. Greene responded that he was not able to do so.

That left Morgan the difficult task of running from Tarleton while avoiding Cornwallis's trap, all the while scrounging for food. The rainy weather made matters even more challenging by swelling the rivers, which made passage over even relatively small creeks time-consuming. Hour after hour, Tarleton's dreaded Legion drew closer. On January 15, as Morgan approached the North Carolina border, he wrote to Greene that he wished to comply with the order to avoid any risky battles "but this will not be always in my power."[56]

By the night of the sixteenth, the trap was closing. Tarleton reached a campground that Morgan had left just that morning, while Cornwallis had advanced to within twenty miles of the Americans from the northeast. The British commanders believed they had the Patriots trapped. Morgan's retreat was blocked by the Broad River, which was so flooded that Morgan would have a tough time crossing it. Knowing this, Tarleton broke camp at 3 A.M. and sent his men on a forced march in hopes of catching the Patriots with half their army stranded on the near side of the river.

Morgan Makes a Stand

Morgan, however, had reached a similar conclusion about his chances of escaping over the flooded river before Tarleton arrived. He saw no choice but to turn around and fight. In fact, he saw the lack of an escape route as

Loyalist Soldiers

The American Revolution was by no means a united effort of colonists against the British government. Throughout the war the number of Americans loyal to the British hovered around five hundred thousand, or anywhere from 20 to 30 percent of the population. Another eighty thousand or so left America for England, Canada, or the West Indies to escape ravages of the war.

The British actively recruited Loyalists, also known as Tories, in all states to fight with them. Unlike the Patriot militias, which tended to remain state militias throughout the war, a number of Loyalist units were incorporated into the regular British army. More than forty battalions were formed from Loyalist volunteers. Some of them were ethnic groups such as the Roman Catholic volunteers formed in 1776 and the Loyal Irish volunteers. Some, such as the King's Rangers, were made up of men from primarily one state, in this case New Jersey. Perhaps the most successful of these units was the Queen's Rangers, formed in August 1776 of recruits from New York, New Jersey, Connecticut, and Virginia. The soldiers drilled and stayed together throughout the war and in 1779 were placed on the regular roll of the British army as the First American Regiment. They fought with Cornwallis's army through most of the Southern campaign.

Despite these troops, however, the British greatly overestimated the support they would receive from Loyalists. In no colony were these people close to being in the majority. In *The War of the American Revolution*, Robert Coakley and Stetson Conn quote Burgoyne as expressing his disillusionment with the American Loyalists and admitting that, contrary to his expectations in New York, "The great bulk of the country is undoubtedly with Congress."

At Cowpens Tarleton (second from right) threw in his cavalry to force the Americans to retreat, but William Washington (center) led a counter attack that broke the British.

an advantage. For although some of his men had been spoiling for a fight and had been miffed with him for retreating, Morgan had seen many cocky soldiers run once the battle started. Now there would be nowhere to run. "Men fight as they deem necessary and no more," Morgan once commented. "When men are forced to fight, they will sell their lives dearly."[57]

He began setting up for battle near a place called Hannah's Cowpens because of its use as a winter pasture for the cattle of local farmers. He chose a section of cleared land and open woods between two creeks. Military experts have criticized the choice because it presented no obstacles to Tarleton's cavalry. But Morgan had come up with a clever plan to turn Tarleton's aggressive tactics against him. The idea was

to play on the British general's arrogance by making victory seem almost laughably easy.

Morgan began spreading his troops in three lines. He placed two small squads of skirmishers in front, one on the left and one on the right. Behind them, he posted the bulk of the militia, with sixty sharpshooters on each side to protect their flank. In a third line, 150 yards to the rear of the militia, he positioned his best troops, Continental soldiers from Maryland and experienced Virginia militia. Hidden behind a ridge to the rear, he stationed Colonel

Morgan's men fire volleys at oncoming British soldiers led by General Tarleton.

William Washington's eighty-five cavalrymen, joined by forty-five horsemen selected from the militia.

Late reinforcements from South Carolina and Georgia had boosted Morgan's numbers to 1,065, nearly the same as Tarleton. Tarleton's soldiers, however, were more experienced, better armed, and more thoroughly trained. They had two cannons (the Americans had none) and more horses. Morgan knew better than to expect his militia troops, most of whom had just shown up for duty without any training at all, to stand firm in the face of cannon fire or a cavalry charge from Tarleton's Legion. Assuming that the militia would break ranks anyway, he designed a way that they could do this without falling into panic. He ordered them to fire three volleys and then retreat behind the

regular army. "By giving them a specific and limited assignment," writes historian Craig Symonds, "Morgan lessened the possibility that they would break and run and in so doing communicate a sense of panic to the regulars."[58] Tarleton, however, would take their action as a sign they were giving up before his invincible troops and might act rashly because of it.

All night long, Morgan mingled with his soldiers, encouraging them with jokes and inspiring them with his quiet confidence. One of his soldiers wrote, "'Just hold up your heads, boys, three fires,' he would say, 'and you are free, and then when you return to your homes, how the old folks will bless you for your gallant conduct.'"[59]

Tarleton's Attack

While the Americans were resting by their campfires, the British marched all through the night. When they reached the Cowpens at dawn on January 17, Tarleton could scarcely believe his good fortune. There was the enemy, formed for battle on ground favorable to attack, their escape cut off by a raging river to their rear. He was aware that most of the enemy troops were militia, and he had no respect for their fighting abilities. True to his impetuous nature, Tarleton formed battle lines without pausing to give his men rest. He placed the Seventh Regiment of infantry on the right, the Seventy-first on the left, and positioned his cavalry on the flanks and rear. As soon as the lines were formed, they rushed forward with a shout.

The Americans responded with shouts of their own. The picket line laid down a blanket of fire and then retreated. The militia and sharpshooters, under the command of Colonel Pickens, then performed their duty. Their three volleys of fire did not slow the British charge, but they picked off a high number of British officers, whose leadership would soon be sorely missed. The militia then retreated in orderly fashion.

The British failed to notice the orderly nature of the retreat. Believing they had already routed the Americans with barely an effort, they surged forward. Some of them on the right flank ran headlong into a charge by Washington's cavalry and were driven back.

The others ran into a solid line of resistance at the center of the line under the leadership of Lieutenant Colonel John Howard. These American troops directed accurate and continuous fire against the enemy.

Confusion in Orders

Tarleton reacted by throwing his cavalry reserve into action. Seeing that this put his right flank in peril, Howard ordered a charge on his right. In the confusion of battle, however, the order got mixed up. Some of the soldiers thought they were supposed to retreat, and, as they did so, others who had not heard the orders began to follow them. Before long, all the rest of Howard's

South Carolina Guerrillas

When the American Continental army in the South fell into disarray, the only active resistance to the British in South Carolina were small roving bands who specialized in hit-and-run activity known as guerrilla warfare. The two most famous leaders of such groups were Francis Marion and Thomas Sumter.

Marion was a respected local citizen and officer who barely escaped Charleston when it fell to the British in 1780. The forty-eight-year old Marion formed a highly disciplined group of horsemen who carried out raids on British supply lines and Loyalist communities in an area between the Santee and Pee Dee Rivers. The British were so annoyed by his activities that they sent the dreaded Banastre Tarleton to teach him a lesson. Tarleton, however, could never pin down Marion, who disappeared into the swamps and forests after each raid.

While Tarleton was futilely chasing after Marion, Sumter stepped up his activities with slightly larger force to the east, closer to the main British army.

Cornwallis finally called Tarleton back to deal with Sumter, who was popularly known as the "Gamecock." Tarleton was so frustrated by Marion that he welcomed the order. In *The War of the American Revolution*, Coakley and Conn quote him as saying, "Let us go back and we will find the Gamecock. But as for this damned old fox [Marion], the devil himself could not catch him." The legend of the man who then became known as the "Swamp Fox" helped bolster Patriot spirits at a time when they were at a low ebb.

Sumter was not nearly as successful. He could often recruit larger forces than Marion by offering to pay them in plunder taken from the British and Loyalists. But his knowledge of military tactics was weak, and several times his troops were caught by surprise and suffered bloody defeats. Nonetheless, he, too, retained popular support and caused enough trouble that Cornwallis, quoted in the Army War College's "The Battle of Cowpens," once said of him, "He certainly has been our greatest plague in this country."

men, seeing the retreat on the flank, assumed that a retreat had been ordered. They, too, began to fall back. As the American line broke, the British, sensing victory, roared in triumph. They rushed forward, breaking their ranks in their eagerness to finish off the defeated Americans.

Morgan was stunned and dismayed at the behavior of his best troops. He had expected them to hold fast, and here they were running off after a brief fight. But when he rushed to head them off, he discovered that they had not been beaten; they believed they had been ordered to withdraw for some strategic reason. Quickly, Morgan and his officers saw how he could turn this misunderstanding to advantage.

"They [the British] are coming on like a mob," said William Washington. "Give them one fire and I'll charge them."[60] Morgan had no trouble rallying his men. He told them they had only to deliver one volley and the battle was theirs. But first, he ordered them to continue their retreat to lead the British on.

Stunning Turnaround

The British surged over the crest of a ridge, believing they were mopping up as part of a spectacular victory. But as they closed to within thirty yards of the Americans, they ran into the last thing they expected to see—a line of determined defenders. The fleeing Americans had suddenly turned. Now they poured a deadly volley into their ranks and then followed with a bayonet charge.

The shock of seeing victory evaporate and the enemy charging them with renewed energy totally deflated the British. Many of them fled in panic or dropped their weapons. Tarleton's cavalry had just begun their charge when suddenly they saw their infantry racing toward them in headlong panic. Despair spread to the horsemen, who had never before encountered stiff resistance and had not expected any. Tarleton tried to rally them, but most refused to respond to orders. Meanwhile, Pickens had reformed his militia, and they charged the British left. Washington's cavalry raced in from the other side. The Americans closed in from all sides and soon had the enemy's main force surrounded.

Tarleton finally rallied a small group of cavalry and desperately tried to mount a counterattack. But after a brief, intense fight with Washington's cavalry, they were driven off. Tarleton was fortunate to escape, along with fourteen officers and forty horsemen. But he left his reputation and most of his army in tatters on the field of battle. Most of his once-dreaded legion of 550 horsemen were either dead or captured. Both infantry regiments he had commanded were destroyed. At the Battle of Cowpens, the British suffered losses of 110 (including 39 officers), 229 wounded, and had 525 taken prisoner. They also lost 100 horses, both cannons, 35 wagons filled with supplies, and 800 muskets. The cost to the Americans was only 12 killed and 60 wounded.

Brilliant but Lucky

In retrospect, Morgan's strategy was brilliant, but he was also extremely lucky. His use of the militia allowed them to contribute in a useful way to the fight and retreat without causing panic. But even so, the Americans likely would have suffered a disastrous defeat were it not for the misunderstanding of orders among the Continental regulars. At the time the error occurred, Howard's men were in a bad situation. They were outnumbered roughly two-to-one by the British and were

American forces drive the British back with bayonets during the Battle of Cowpens.

about to be outflanked by Tarleton's cavalry. Furthermore, the two British cannons were being moved into position to fire on them. Had they stayed where they were and fought, they likely would have been overwhelmed. The American militia, left on their own without the professionals to anchor them, would then have been captured. The retreat, although not ordered, was exactly what the

Blacks in the American Revolution

At the time of the American Revolution, slavery was so firmly established that at least 25 percent of the colonists owned slaves. More than half of these were concentrated in the colonies of Virginia and Maryland. Although most of the rest lived in the South, slaves were not unknown on New York and Pennsylvania farms.

Because most blacks were slaves, a small percentage of them served in the American armies. There were cases in which slaves were offered freedom in exchange for their military service, but most of these fought on the Loyalist side. In fact, the British actively recruited slaves of Patriots with offers of freedom, and this tended to solidify support for the Patriot cause in slave-owning areas. Support for the Loyalist cause in Virginia, for example, dwindled considerably after Lord Dunmore, governor of the colony, called on slaves to revolt against their Patriot masters.

There were, however, a significant number of free blacks who fought on the Patriot side.

Dupuy and Dupuy, in *An Outline History of the American Revolution*, quote a traveler as writing: "At the ferry-crossing I met with a detachment of the Rhode Island regime. . . . The majority of the enlisted men were black or mulattos; but they are strong robust men, and those I saw made a very good appearance." The Dupuys observe that blacks tended to stay with the cause and serve longer terms of duty than white militia.

Among the African American heroes of the Patriot cause were Crispus Attucks, a victim of the Boston Massacre in 1770; Peter Salem, who joined his fellow Patriots in standing up against the British at Lexington; and an unnamed aide to Lieutenant Colonel William Washington. John Marshall described an incident, related on the website www.pbs.org, in which "a waiter, too small to wield a sword," saved Washington's life at the Battle of Cowpens. The aide shot a British cavalryman with his pistol just as he was about to slash Washington.

Americans needed to get them out of a dangerous situation. The fact that they retreated before they were beaten allowed them to withdraw in such fine order and spirits that they had no trouble reforming and turning on the British. It was this quick reforming that caught the British by surprise and caused them to panic instead.

Morgan deflected all credit from himself and passed it along to his men. "Our success must be attributed to the justice of our cause and the gallantry of our troops," he said. "My wishes would induce me to name every sentinel in the corps."[61]

In contrast, the British officers put the entire blame for the loss on the performance of their soldiers, while Tarleton managed to avoid any criticism from his superiors for his handling of the battle. Cornwallis publicly endorsed Tarleton's entire plan of action. He comforted the defeated commander by writing, "The total misbehavior of the troops could alone have deprived you of the glory which was so justly your due."[62] However, Tarleton's rash, overly aggressive actions were what put his army in the position where they could be surprised and then overwhelmed by the enemy.

Consequences of Cowpens

After the Battle of Cowpens, a stunned General Cornwallis wrote, "It is impossible to foresee all the consequences that this unexpected event may produce."[63] It turned out that the effect of the Battle of Cowpens was as dramatic as the victory at Kings Mountain just two months earlier. Had Tarleton won, the already weakened American army in the South would have been crippled, possibly beyond repair. Without any effective force to counter British activity, the Americans would have had to cede the entire South to the British. Cornwallis would have been able to march in relative security up into North Carolina and on to Virginia. Tarleton would have remained a feared, almost legendary character and would have struck fear into American resistance wherever he encountered it. As it happened, Tarleton was never again a significant player in the war. Although Cornwallis refused to criticize him for his leadership at Cowpens, he never again assigned Tarleton a significant command.

Instead, Cornwallis had again lost his entire left flank. The combined losses at the Battle of Kings Mountain and Cowpens deprived him of two thousand soldiers, that he could not replace. The end result was that Cornwallis gave up on the Southern strategy. In defiance of Clinton's wishes, he made no further attempt to pacify or gain control of the Southern colonies. Instead, stubbornly, he insisted on continuing his drive to the North, even

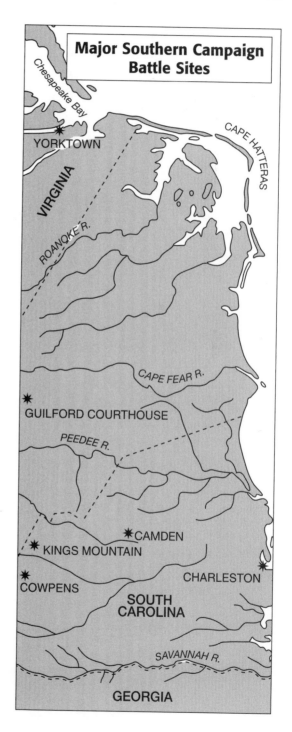

Major Southern Campaign Battle Sites

Chesapeake Bay

CAPE HATTERAS

YORKTOWN

VIRGINIA

ROANOKE R.

CAPE FEAR R.

GUILFORD COURTHOUSE

PEEDEE R.

CAMDEN

KINGS MOUNTAIN

CHARLESTON

COWPENS

SOUTH CAROLINA

SAVANNAH R.

GEORGIA

though that was supposed to have been done after gaining control of the South. "Nothing but the most absolute necessity shall induce me to give up the important objective of the winter's campaign," he wrote, referring to his move into North Carolina. "Defensive measures would be certain ruin to the affairs of Britain in the southern colonies."[64]

As it turned out, his pursuit of his winter objective would lead to the most ruinous outcome for the British of the entire war.

Chapter 8

Yorktown

In 1779 and 1780, George Washington had managed to keep his army in the field, but just barely. His Continental army did not see any significant action in either of those years, and that was probably to their benefit. Following the initial enthusiasm for the rebellion and the spurts of ardor that followed the victories at Saratoga and Trenton, the rebellion had been fizzling out. Even with French assistance, the Americans had neither the manpower nor the financial means to fight Great Britain. The long war had dragged down the colonial economy and forced hard times on all. The Continental army had no uniforms and poor supplies, and most of its soldiers had not been paid in many months. Although the British had withdrawn from Philadelphia, they still held New York City. Much as he wished to evict them, Washington's scruffy army of 3,500 soldiers had no chance of ousting the 14,500 regulars under the command of Henry Clinton. In April 1781, the American general wrote that he was at the end of his rope. He kept his faint hopes pinned on Great Britain's dissatisfaction with the costly war, hopes which were kept afloat by the Americans' stunning victories in the South. In April 1781 Washington believed that both sides were so war weary that the next major military breakthrough for either side could decide the war.

Cornwallis Moves North

Meanwhile the defeats at Kings Mountain and Cowpens and an even bloodier, though inconclusive, battle at Guilford Courthouse had taken their toll on General Cornwallis's spirits and his confidence. With single-minded determination, he abandoned the untamed colonies to the south and began focusing instead on Virginia, the largest and wealthiest of the colonies. In the words of historian Robert Middlekauff, "He was tired from the long and depressing campaign, and he was looking for excuses for his abandonment of the Carolinas. He was also looking for direction."[65]

The Battle of Guilford Courthouse

Although the Battle of Guilford Courthouse was technically an American defeat, it marked one of the best performances by the Continental army in open battle against the British during the entire war.

After Morgan rejoined his army, and strengthened by further recruits, Nathanael Greene decided to take on the British at Guilford Courthouse in North Carolina. He copied Morgan's strategy for victory at Cowpens, placing his forces in three lines of defense with the raw North Carolina militia in front. The second line was composed of Virginia militia, placed in a thick forest to conceal them and break up the tight British attack formations. Greene's Continental army troops waited in the rear.

The British apparently learned nothing from Cowpens. Again, on March 15, 1781, they threw their troops into battle directly after an exhausting twelve-mile march. The North Carolina militia got in a deadly volley on the advancing British lines and then raced to the cover of the woods. The British marched on and ran into fierce resistance in the woods from the Virginia troops.

After a half hour of taking heavy losses, the British finally drove the Americans from the woods. They continued to advance, expecting they had cleared the enemy from the battlefield, only to encounter the best American troops. The fighting was intense, but gradually the Continentals gained the upper hand. At one point, Cornwallis, seeing his troops were being overrun, resorted to the desperate measure of firing an artillery barrage right into the thickest part of the battle. The deadly fire killed British as well as American soldiers, but it stopped the American momentum. Greene then ordered a retreat, and the Americans left the field to the British. According to the rules of war, this conceded victory to the British. But with 93 dead and 439 wounded, Cornwallis had lost more than a quarter of his army in the field. Against this, the Americans counted 78 killed and 183 wounded. With his army now in desperate shape, Cornwallis had to retreat all the way to the east Carolina coast for reinforcements.

Cornwallis's move surprised and irritated his superior, General Clinton. Clinton was not pleased that Cornwallis had apparently failed to accomplish his goal of subduing the South, and was now, without consulting anyone, giving up on the project altogether. The fact that Cornwallis was moving into Clinton's area of command further strained their relations. Nonetheless, Clinton cooperated with Cornwallis's drive to stamp out rebellion in Virginia. He sent a force of eighteen hundred under Benedict Arnold, who had turned traitor and was now fighting for the British, to burn the city of Richmond. When Washington sent General Lafayette with twelve hundred men to fight him, Clinton responded by dispatching another twenty-six hundred troops under Major General William Phillips to the area. These forces joined together with Cornwallis to form an army of close to nine thousand men.

Lafayette received reinforcements from the Virginia militia, but even that was not enough to allow him to challenge the British in battle. Yet he had to do something to satisfy the Virginia men who were fuming at seeing the British burning their cities and homes. "I am determined to skirmish but not to engage too far,"[66] said Lafayette, as he hovered just out of striking range of the

British. Cornwallis tired of chasing him and turned his attention toward capturing the Virginia assembly in Charlottesville. Such statesmen as Thomas Jefferson narrowly escaped before the British arrived.

On June 10, Lafayette was joined by General Wayne and some West Virginia militia, whose reinforcements boosted his army to nearly five thousand. This allowed Lafayette to be bolder in his challenge. He advanced cautiously to the south and engaged in a skirmish with British forces on June 26 at Williamsburg.

Washington Versus Clinton in New York

Further north, Washington and Clinton were locked in a battle of wits over New York. Washington desperately wanted to drive the British out of that city but lacked the military strength to do it. However, in May, he received word that the French admiral de Grasse was planning to bring his powerful fleet up from its base in the Caribbean to escape the approaching hurricane season. This seemed like the chance Washington had been waiting for. The combination of his five-thousand- man army, the four thousand French troops under General Rochambeau stationed in nearby Newport, Rhode Island, and the French fleet would give him the strength to attempt an attack. Observing Clinton's strength in New York, Rochambeau doubted that it was wise to try. But he yielded to Washington as the supreme commander and marched south to join him.

Clinton viewed Washington's growing strength with alarm and began to suspect that the Americans and French were planning a major attack. Suddenly, he regretted having weakened his army to aid Cornwallis's Virginia campaign. He sent word to Cornwallis to send back three thousand men.

French general Lafayette was instrumental in helping to defeat the British in the last years of the war.

The order infuriated Cornwallis, but he had no choice but to obey his superior officer. He left Williamsburg and began crossing the James River on the way east to Portsmouth, where the requested soldiers could be loaded on ships sailing for New

General Rochambeau, the commander of French forces in America, advised Washington against an attack on New York.

York. Spotting the movement, Lafayette thought it was a golden opportunity to catch the British off guard. When he thought that half the British force was across the river, he sent five hundred men under General Wayne to attack the remaining troops on the near side of the river. Lafayette badly misjudged, however. Cornwallis had sent only his baggage across by the time Wayne attacked, leaving the small American force to contend with his entire army. Wayne's forces took a terrible beating and barely managed to avoid destruction by fighting their way out of encirclement with bayonets.

Meanwhile, Washington's plans for taking New York had crumbled. He spent most of July and part of August hunting for a weak spot in Clinton's defenses before finally admitting he could find none. On August 14, his last hopes fizzled when he received word from de Grasse that the French fleet was sailing for the Chesapeake Bay, not New York, and that they would be there only until mid-October before returning to the Caribbean.

Clinton sensed that his enemy had at least temporarily shelved plans for an attack. With the immediate threat removed, Clinton then reversed his order and told Cornwallis not to send the troops. Instead, he advised Cornwallis to establish a strong base at some deep water seaport on the Virginia coast where they could be in close contact with the British fleet. Cornwallis chose to occupy an old tobacco port known as Yorktown, on the Atlantic coast south of the York River.

A Golden Opportunity

Washington's dejection at his lost opportunity in New York turned to optimism when he recognized the alternative opportunity that the French and British movements had provided. Clinton's ill-advised order had sent Cornwallis backing himself into the northeast corner of Virginia. If the French fleet was indeed going to be in the Chesapeake Bay, they could drive off the British ships and seal Cornwallis in. If a strong army approached from the west, it could trap the British and perhaps force their surrender.

But where would that strong army come from? Lafayette did not have the numbers to threaten Cornwallis, nor could he expect adequate help from the American forces in the south. Their only chance to trap Cornwallis lay in Washington bringing his army down to do it. That, however, posed an enormous risk. Once Clinton recognized Washington's plan, he could follow him down to Virginia. With his ability to transport troops quickly on British ships, he could beat Washington to any point he chose. The likely result was that Washington would find himself either caught on the run or trapped between Clinton and Cornwallis. Furthermore, the plan depended on exact timing. De Grasse had said that he planned to head back to the West Indies by mid-October. Once de Grasse sailed away, there would be nothing to prevent Cornwallis from loading his army on ships and escaping. That gave Washington less than two months to march his army 450 miles and force the surrender of a formidable

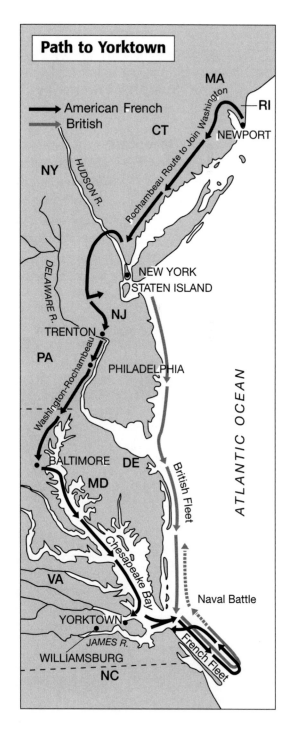

Path to Yorktown

American French
British

MA
RI
NEWPORT

Rochambeau Route to Join Washington

CT

NY

HUDSON R.

DELAWARE R.

NEW YORK
STATEN ISLAND

NJ

TRENTON

PA

Washington-Rochambeau

PHILADELPHIA

ATLANTIC OCEAN

BALTIMORE

DE

MD

British Fleet

Chesapeake Bay

VA

Naval Battle

YORKTOWN

JAMES R.

WILLIAMSBURG

French Fleet

NC

army, or the whole adventure would be for naught. And even if they accomplished that, the plan would fail unless de Grasse was able to defeat the British fleet, generally regarded as the best in the world.

Deception

Washington decided it was worth the risk as long as he took careful steps to conceal his intentions from Clinton until the last possible moment. That meant taking an even greater risk. He left Major General William Heath with only twenty-five hundred men to present the illusion that the Americans were still camped outside of New York. Clinton

General Cornwallis chose to occupy Yorktown and Washington carefully contrived to force his surrender.

could annihilate such a small force if he became aware of its weakness. Meanwhile, on August 21, Washington and Rochambeau began a swift march with two thousand Americans and four thousand Frenchmen to the south.

The Americans and French went to great lengths to hide their movements from Clinton. Just prior to leaving, they ordered huge baking ovens to be built at the French camp, which the British took as a sure sign that the French planned to establish their base there for many weeks to come. The Americans allowed false orders, which spoke of a renewed American effort to attack New York, to fall into British hands.

The deceptions worked. Even when Clinton's scouts reported a movement of American and French troops to the south, Clinton believed it was just a feint to mask their true intentions to attack New York. As a result, he made no move to either follow Washington southward or to attack Heath, and he declined to send any support to Cornwallis. By the time Clinton realized what had happened, it was too late for him to act. For his part, Heath was able to withdraw from harm's way. When Clinton wrote to Cornwallis on September 2 to warn him that the Americans were heading south, Washington's army was already in Philadelphia.

Cornwallis greeted the news of Washington's approach with little concern. Unaware that the French fleet was entering the picture, he saw no reason to fear Washington. Clinton, Cornwallis believed, could

The French and British fleets engage in battle on the seas off the Virginia coast.

send reinforcements by ship whenever he pleased, and if worse came to worst, his forces could simply evacuate Yorktown by ship. As a result, he spent little effort on building up defensive positions.

The French Fleet

The key to the entire American plan was the fate of the French fleet. On August 5, de Grasse sailed from Cap François in the Caribbean with twenty-eight warships and thirty-three hundred soldiers. British admiral Sir Samuel Hood, who had been keeping

an eye on the French fleet, learned of its departure and sailed north with fourteen ships to follow it. However, since they were unable to make contact with the French, they could only guess where de Grasse was headed. There seemed to be just two possibilities: the Chesapeake Bay to cause trouble for Cornwallis or New York to join an attack on Clinton.

Hood sped north and arrived in Chesapeake Bay on August 25. Seeing no sign of any French ships, he concluded that the enemy's destination was New York, and he set sail to meet them there. Unknown to him, however, de Grasse had stopped at the port of Havana and was actually well behind

Hood. By the time the French fleet arrived at the Chesapeake Bay on August 30, Hood was long gone. Still confused as to the French plan, Hood turned around and sailed back to Chesapeake Bay, arriving there on September 5.

✗ Desperate to keep the British fleet distracted so that they would not threaten Admiral de Barras's squadron that was sailing from Newport with siege artillery for the campaign against Cornwallis, de Grasse sailed out to sea to challenge the British. The two navies fought one fierce but brief battle and then spent five days maneuvering for position. By September 10, de Barras's small squadron had slipped in past the British and, having unloaded their cargo, now joined de Grasse. Unable to challenge a French fleet that now numbered thirty-five ships, the British had to sail back to New York, leaving the French in complete control of Chesapeake Bay.

Cornwallis in a Corner

The Americans' only concern now was whether Lafayette's army, reinforced by de Grasse, was strong enough to keep Cornwallis from breaking out until Washington and Rochambeau arrived. But Cornwallis made no effort to fight his way out of the closing trap. He had been ordered to this position by Clinton, and he expected his superior would come through with reinforcements. "If I had no hopes of relief," he explained, "I would rather risk action than defend my half-finished works. But as you say Admiral Digby [of the British fleet] is hourly expected, and

promises me every exertion to assist me, I do not think myself justified in putting the fate of the War on so desperate an Attempt."[67]

Washington and Rochambeau arrived in Williamsburg on September 14, but they had marched so speedily that it took ten days for the last of the stragglers to catch up. On September 28, the Americans and French marched to Yorktown. The American army took up positions south of Yorktown and the French to the west, while the Virginia militia set up on the north bank of the York to block any possible escape across the river. Now Cornwallis and his eighty-eight hundred troops were hemmed in by fifteen thousand American and French soldiers.

Race Against Time

In Washington's mind only one thing could prevent his plan from working: de Grasse. If the French admiral stuck to his plan to return to the Caribbean at the end of September, their great opportunity would be lost. De Grasse agreed to stay a few weeks longer, but that meant Washington had to get busy and force a surrender. Fortunately for him, Cornwallis played right into his hands. Still counting on a massive relief effort from Clinton, the British general pulled his army back into a tight defensive formation around Yorktown. That protective measure has been widely criticized by historians, for by doing so, the British gave up ground that would have taken the Americans and French perhaps two weeks to gain by force.

In the first week of October, the Americans and their French allies closed in. On

October 6, they began digging a long line of trenches nearer the British front lines. Their heavy siege cannons opened fire and bombarded the British day and night. Low on ammunition, Cornwallis's men could do little to fight back. The bombardment slowly took its toll in casualties, damage, and psychological strain. To make matters worse, a severe outbreak of smallpox spread throughout the camp.

Cornwallis realized that he was now in serious trouble. On October 10, he wrote, "Nothing but a direct move to the York River which includes a successful naval action can save us."[68] Meanwhile, the allies continued to tighten their grip. On October 11, they forced the British outer defenses to pull back yet again and constructed another series of trenches.

Frantic Measures

While Cornwallis was frantically pleading for help, Clinton at last realized the peril that surrounded his general. He began grasping for some way to put together a rescue mission. But in order to transport his reinforcements to Yorktown, he needed cooperation from the navy, and he did not get it. Admiral Thomas Graves insisted that his fleet, battered in their engagement with de Grasse,

Naval Battle of the Capes

Having discovered that the French fleet was not in the New York area, the British fleet of nineteen ships under Admiral Thomas Graves returned to Chesapeake Bay, arriving on September 5, 1781. There they found Admiral de Grasse and the twenty-eight ships of the French fleet. Concerned that the British might stumble upon another French fleet that was transporting siege artillery from New York and destroy it, de Grasse chose to meet the British in the open water of the Atlantic.

Seeing the French fleet emerging from the bay, the British turned sharply to meet it. In doing so, they reversed the order of their ships. This put the cautious Graves at the front of the line in charge of the battle, rather than the more aggressive Admiral Samuel Hood. Rather than attacking the French fleet before the ships could get organized, Graves sailed on a parallel course for an hour. Following the standard, conservative British naval battle procedure, he ordered the ship to stay in a line broadside to the French, even though his enemy had superior firepower.

The two lines of ships approached each other at a thirty degree angle. This meant that only the forward ships were engaged in the early fighting. In fact, only eight British ships and fifteen French vessels saw significant action.

The two-hour battle did not produce a clear winner. Although several ships on both sides suffered severe damage, only one ship (British) was so badly battered that it sank two days later. However, the consequences of the affair were disastrous for the British. The battle so distracted the British that the French were able to sail their siege artillery down the bay and into position at Yorktown without any problem. The French fleet remained in control of the bay, and the addition of these eight ships gave the French such overwhelming naval superiority that the British could not risk another battle to dislodge them. The British fleet had no choice but to return to New York. Several of its ships were so badly shot up that they required extensive repairs, which took so long to complete that the fleet was never able to mount another rescue attempt on behalf of Cornwallis.

needed to complete repairs before they could sail back into battle. Not until October 13 did he declare the fleet ready to sail. At that point, there might still have been time to rescue Cornwallis, but a large storm blew in as Clinton's relief force was preparing to leave and forced another delay.

The British defenses at Yorktown now depended upon two heavily fortified hills, known as redoubts, just outside the city. The allies executed a nighttime attack, with the French attacking one hill and the Americans the other. One American commander, Alexander Hamilton, broke the tension of battle when he led the Americans in a lighthearted competition with the French. Upon capturing the redoubt,

he sent a message to Rochambeau, teasing, "I am in my redoubt. Where are you?" Rochambeau fired back, "Tell the marquis I am not in mine but will be in five minutes."[69] The Frenchman made good on his promise. With control of the two redoubts, the allies could now haul their siege guns within 250 yards of the British compound.

Frustrated by Cornwallis's passivity, his officers argued in favor of a breakout attempt. Recognizing the odds against him, Cornwallis was unenthusiastic. When he finally gave approval, it was only for a token ef-

French and American artillerymen shell the British positions at Yorktown.

French Aid

The American victory in the Revolutionary War owed a great deal to the aid that the French government provided. The French sided with the Americans not out of any great admiration for the colonists or American ideals of independence but as part of a long-standing political conflict with Great Britain. The French had been humiliated by their defeat in the Seven Years' War, which had resulted in their being kicked out of North America.

Some officials in France had recognized immediately after their defeat in that war the potential problems that the British faced in their colonies. At that time they began planning how to aid the colonies militarily. The main military step was rebuilding their navy so that it could contend with the British in the Caribbean Sea and on the Atlantic Coast.

When the war began in 1775, France officially stayed neutral. But according to Dupuy and Dupuy, in *An Outline History of the American Revolution,* secret memos in France advocated providing secret aid to the Americans "without making any convention with them until their independence be established and notorious." Spain and the Netherlands, who, like France, had no great love for the British, joined in a scheme of providing secret aid. Supplies such as weapons and ammunitions were purchased in the Netherlands and shipped to French and Dutch possessions in the West Indies. From there, the goods were transferred to American blockade runners, who smuggled them into the colonies. A few French individuals, most notably Marquis de Lafayette, volunteered to fight with the Americans and paid their own expenses to do so.

Continuing aid from France depended, however, on the Americans showing they could put up a good fight against the British. In that regard, George Washington's greatest service was in keeping enough of an army together and achieving just enough success on the battlefield to justify France providing aid.

In March 1777, France formally declared its support for the colonies, beginning with a massive interest-free loan. Over the next four years France sent more than sixteen thousand troops to fight against the British on the North American continent. They generally conducted themselves with a courtesy and civility that was in stark contrast to the atrocities that raged between Patriots and Loyalists. When France began taking a more open stance on the side of the colonies, Washington used it as a recruiting tool. He repeatedly stressed the shame that would fall on America if the French showed such a willingness to fight for them and yet the cause failed because the Americans failed to show the gumption to fight for themselves.

Not all the French ventures in the war were successful, a failed attack on Savannah being the prime example. But Rochambeau's army was helpful in keeping Clinton at bay in New York for much of the later war, and the French army and navy played major roles in the capture of Cornwallis at Yorktown.

fort. Only 350 British soldiers charged the allied lines. Their surprise attack achieved modest success—they captured a handful of prisoners and put six cannons out of action before withdrawing. But it was nowhere near enough to loosen the noose that the allies were closing.

Cornwallis's last hope was a bold scheme to send his army across the river under the cover of darkness to Gloucester Point, where only the Virginia militia and about 750 French soldiers barred their way to freedom. With luck, they could march north to rejoin Clinton. On the night of October 16, his

The British surrender their entire force at Yorktown, effectively ending the Revolutionary War.

army stealthily began boarding sixteen flatboats. He got all of his wounded and more than one thousand soldiers across on the first trip. But as the second group shoved off for the two-hour round trip, the weather again proved their worst enemy. A fierce storm blew in and battered the small flotilla. Although they rowed with all their might, they could make little progress against the wind and returned to shore exhausted. By the time the storm had abated, it was too late to get the army across. Cornwallis had no choice but to order those who had already crossed to return.

Out of Options

Now Cornwallis realized his cause was hopeless. His artillery shells were gone, all his defensive works had been destroyed, and he was losing men to the relentless allied artillery barrage. At 11 A.M. on October 19, he sent a messenger to the enemy camp that read, "Sir, I propose a cessation of hostility for twenty-four hours, and that two officers may be appointed by each side . . . to settle terms for the surrender of the posts at York and Gloucester."[70]

Cornwallis avoided public humiliation by staying in camp and sending representatives out to meet with the allied forces at 2 P.M. Still reluctant to consider the Americans more than a band of rebels, the British officers tried to surrender to the French, but General Rochambeau declined, "We are subordinate to the Americans,"[71] he said. Washington accepted the surrender of 8,885 British soldiers, by far the largest surrender of the war. Although he had initially resisted the plan, once he recognized the possible rewards, he had carried out the strategy flawlessly. Cornwallis and Clinton could only blame themselves for having unnecessarily put such a large army into a position from which it could be trapped and captured.

"It Is All Over!"

Upon hearing the news from Yorktown, British king George III declared it a mere setback and resolved to carry on the fight. But most British officials shared the reaction of Britain's prime minister, Lord North, who exclaimed, "Oh God! It is all over!"[72] Few members of the government had any appetite for continuing the war, especially now that they had lost control of the South completely. No significant fighting would occur in the American Revolution following Cornwallis's surrender, although negotiations dragged on for many months. On September 3, 1783, nearly two years after Yorktown, the treaty documents were finally signed, ending the war and leaving the American colonies free and independent.

☆ Notes ☆

Introduction: Former Friends– Different Stategies

1. Quoted in W.P. Cumming and Hugh Rankin, *The Fate of a Nation*. London: Phaedon Press, 1975, p. 14.
2. Quoted in Benson Bobrick, *Angel in the Whirlwind: The Triumph of the American Revolution*. New York: Simon & Schuster, 1997, p. 74.
3. Quoted in Bobrick, *Angel in the Whirlwind*, p. 87.
4. Quoted in Cumming and Rankin, *The Fate of a Nation*, p. 33.
5. Quoted in Russell B. Adams, *The American Story: The Revolutionaries*. Alexandria, VA: Time-Life Books, 1996, p. 33.

Chapter 1: Bunker Hill

6. Quoted in Bobrick, *Angel in the Whirlwind*, p. 140.
7. Quoted in Cumming and Rankin, *The Fate of a Nation*, p. 50.
8. Quoted in Henry B. Carrington, *Battles of the American Revolution*. New York: Promontory Press, 1881, p. 93.
9. Quoted in Bobrick, *Angel in the Whirlwind*, p. 140.
10. Quoted in Adams, *The American Story*, p. 50.
11. Quoted in Robert Middlekauff, *The Glorious Cause: The American Revolution,*

1763–1789. New York: Oxford, 1982, p. 288.
12. Quoted in Bobrick, *Angel in the Whirlwind*, p. 141.
13. Quoted in Carrington, *Battles of the American Revolution*, p. 108.
14. W. J. Wood, *Battles of the Revolutionary War, 1775–1781*. Chapel Hill: University of North Carolina Press, 1990, p. xx.
15. Wood, *Battles of the Revolutionary War*, p. 33.
16. Quoted in Craig L. Symonds, *A Battlefield Atlas of the American Revolution*. Annapolis, MD: Nautical and Aviation Publication Company of America, 1986, p. 19.
17. Quoted in Carrington, *Battles of the American Revolution*, p. 116.

Chapter 2: Quebec

18. Quoted in Bobrick, *Angel in the Whirlwind*, p. 175.
19. Quoted in Cumming and Rankin, *The Fate of a Nation*, p. 69.
20. Quoted in "The Battle of Quebec," theamericanrevolution.org.
21. Quoted in Wood, *Battles of the Revolutionary War*, p. 53.
22. Quoted in Adams, *The American Story*, p. 51.

Chapter 3: Trenton

23. Quoted in Adams, *The American Story,* p. 89.

24. Quoted in Adams, *The American Story,* p. 49.

25. Quoted in Robert Cowley, ed., *What If? The World's Foremost Military Historians Imagine What Might Have Been.* New York: E. P. Putnam's Sons, 1999, p. 164.

26. Quoted in A. J. Langguth, *Patriots: The Men Who Started the American Revolution.* New York: Simon & Schuster, 1988, p. 400.

27. Wood, *Battles of the Revolutionary War,* p. 59.

28. Quoted in John Rhodehamel, ed., *The American Revolution: Writings from the War of Independence.* New York: Library of America, 2001, p. 236.

29. Quoted in Middlekauff, *The Glorious Cause,* p. 357.

30. Quoted in Langguth, *Patriots,* p. 410.

31. Quoted in "The Battle of Trenton." users.rcn.com/gualis/.

32. Quoted in Charles Royster, *A Revolutionary People at War: The Continental Army and the American Character, 1775–1783.* Chapel Hill: University of North Carolina Press, 1979, p. 118.

33. Quoted in Wood, *Battles of the Revolutionary War,* p. 79.

34. Quoted in R. Ernest Dupuy and Trevor N. Dupuy, *An Outline History of the American Revolution.* New York: Harper and Row, 1975, p. 73.

Chapter 4: Saratoga

35. Quoted in Cumming and Rankin, *The Fate of a Nation,* p. 143.

36. Quoted in Bobrick, *Angel in the Whirlwind,* p. 254.

37. Quoted in Symonds, *A Battlefield Atlas of the American Revolution,* p. 45.

38. Quoted in Middlekauff, *The Glorious Cause,* p. 382.

39. Quoted in Cowley, *What If?* p. 171.

40. Symonds, *A Battlefield Atlas of the American Revolution,* p. 36.

Chapter 5: Brandywine

41. Wood, *Battles of the Revolutionary War,* p. 95.

42. Symonds, *A Battlefield Atlas of the American Revolution,* p. 55.

43. Quoted in Wood, *Battles of the Revolutionary War,* p. 107.

44. Quoted in "The Battle of Brandywine." ushistory.org.

45. Quoted in "The Battle of Brandywine."

46. Wood, *Battles of the Revolutionary War,* p. 114.

Chapter 6: Kings Mountain

47. Quoted in Middlekauff, *The Glorious Cause,* p. 423.

48. Quoted in Royster, *A Revolutionary People at War,* p. 271.

49. Quoted in Peggy Beach, "Battle of King's Mountain." www.co:cleve.nc.us.

50. Quoted in General Francis Preston, "Memorial Address." Washington County Historical Society, Abingdon,

Virginia, October 7, 1810. www.tulsa.oklahoma.net.

51. Quoted in Bobrick, *Angel in the Whirlwind,* p. 425.

52. Quoted in Preston, "Memorial Address."

53. Quoted in Preston, "Memorial Address."

Chapter 7: Cowpens

54. Quoted in Army War College, Historical Section, "The Battle of Cowpens." www.ls.net.

55. Quoted in Army War College, "The Battle of Cowpens."

56. Quoted in Army War College, "The Battle of Cowpens."

57. Quoted in Adams, *The American Story,* p. 142.

58. Quoted in Symonds, *A Battlefield Atlas of the American Revolution,* p. 91.

59. Quoted in Langguth, *Patriots,* p. 429.

60. Quoted in Cowley, *What If?* p. 177.

61. Quoted in Army War College, "The Battle of Cowpens."

62. Quoted in Army War College, "The Battle of Cowpens."

63. Quoted in Army War College, "The Battle of Cowpens."

64. Quoted in Army War College, "The Battle of Cowpens."

Chapter 8: Yorktown

65. Middlekauff, *The Glorious Cause,* p. 559.

66. Quoted in Royster, *A Revolutionary People at War,* p. 152.

67. Quoted in Adams, *The American Story,* p. 159.

68. Quoted in Symonds, *A Battlefield Atlas of the American Revolution,* p. 105.

69. Quoted in Langguth, *Patriots,* p. 536.

70. Quoted in Cowley, *What If?* p. 182.

71. Quoted in Symonds, *A Battlefield Atlas of the American Revolution,* p. 107.

72. Quoted in Symonds, *A Battlefield Atlas of the American Revolution,* p. 108.

★ For Further Reading ★

Bruce Bliven, *The American Revolution: 1760–1783*. New York: Random House, 1987. Fast-paced account of the events leading up to the Revolution and the battles that decided it.

Edward F. Dolan, *The American Revolution: How We Fought the War of Independence*. Brookfield, CT: Millbrook Press, 1995. Covers the Revolution from Lexington to Yorktown highlighting historic figures from both sides of the war.

Thomas Fleming, *Liberty! The American Revolution*. New York: Penguin, 1998. A thoroughly documented history of the American Revolution that includes many color illustrations and fascinating insights into life during those years.

Webb B. Garrison, *Great Stories of the American Revolution*. Danbury, CT: Rutledge Hill Press, 1993. Captures the flavor of the period with short, dramatic stories.

Joy Hakim, *From Colonies to Country*. New York: Oxford University Press, 1993. Probably the liveliest history of the Revolution, this book makes the war come alive and addresses the roles of women, blacks, Indians, and others.

Albert Marrin, *The War of Independence: The Story of the American Revolution*. New York: Atheneum, 1998. A detailed look at the Revolutionary War. The author concentrates on the military aspects of the Revolution.

✫ Works Consulted ✫

Books

Russell B. Adams, *The American Story: The Revolutionaries*. Alexandria, VA: Time-Life Books, 1996. History of the American Revolution with an emphasis on biographical material.

Mark Mayo Boatner III, *Encyclopedia of the American Revolution*. New York: David McKay and Company, 1974. Short entries give brief explanations of many aspects of the war.

Benson Bobrick, *Angel in the Whirlwind: The Triumph of the American Revolution*. New York: Simon & Schuster, 1997. Probably the most readable, informative account of the Revolution, this book uses a dramatic narrative style that covers a great deal of information about the war.

Henry B. Carrington, *Battles of the American Revolution*. New York: Promontory Press, 1881. Detailed and often difficult reading, this book, which is more than a century old, gives the perspective of an author closer to the actual era of the war.

Robert Coakley and Stetson Conn, *The War of the American Revolution*. Washington, DC: Center of Military History of the United States Army, 1975. A slightly more technical view of the military events of the Revolution.

Robert Cowley, ed., *What If? The World's Foremost Military Historians Imagine What Might Have Been*. New York: E.P. Putnam's Sons, 1999. A fascinating book that asks noted historians to speculate on what would have happened had minor incidents not occurred. It includes a section on the many points at which the American cause hung in the balance during the Revolution.

W.P. Cumming and Hugh Rankin, *The Fate of a Nation*. London: Phaedon Press, 1975. This book examines the American Revolution through the writings of the actual participants.

R. Ernest Dupuy and Trevor N. Dupuy, *An Outline History of the American Revolution*. New York: Harper and Row, 1975. A more abbreviated history for those looking for an overview.

A.J. Langguth, *Patriots: The Men Who Started the American Revolution*. New York: Simon & Schuster, 1988. Fairly straightforward biographical treatment.

Robert Middlekauff, *The Glorious Cause: The American Revolution, 1763–1789*. New York: Oxford, 1982. One of the longer, more detailed histories of the war.

David Ramsey, *The Life of George Washington*. Baltimore, MD: C.I. Thomas, 1807. The earliest biography of Washington, published just eight years after his death.

John Rhodehamel, ed., *The American Revolution: Writings from the War of Independence.* New York: Library of America, 2001. This book uses all primary sources in telling the story of the Revolutionary War.

Charles Royster, *A Revolutionary People at War: The Continental Army and the American Character, 1775–1783.* Chapel Hill: University of North Carolina Press, 1979. A nontraditional history probes the thoughts and emotions that influenced those who participated in the war.

Craig L. Symonds, *A Battlefield Atlas of the American Revolution.* Annapolis, MD: Nautical and Aviation Publication Company of America, 1986. This book focuses strictly on the actual battles and includes helpful battlefield maps.

Anthony F.C. Wallace, *The Long Bitter Trail: Andrew Jackson and the Indians.* New York: Hill and Wang, 1993. This book contains background on the situation of American Indians in Revolutionary War times.

W. J. Wood, *Battles of the Revolutionary War, 1775–1781.* Chapel Hill: University of North Carolina Press, 1990. Treats the battles of the Revolution in great detail.

Internet Sources

Army War College, Historical Section, "The Battle of Cowpens." www.ls.net.

"The Battle of Brandywine." ushistory.org.

"The Battle of Quebec." theamerican revolution.org.

"The Battle of Trenton." users.rcn.com/gualis/.

Peggy Beach, "Battle of King's Mountain." www.co:cleve.nc.us.

Edward J. Lowell, *The Hessians.* www.american revolution.org.

General Francis Preston, "Memorial Address," Washington County Historical Society, Abingdon, Virginia, October 7, 1810. www.tulsa.oklahoma.net.

Robert W. Williams, "General Joseph Warren." www.warrentavern.com.

Website
Public Broadcasting System (www.pbs.org).

☆ Index ☆

★ Picture Credits ★

Cover Photo: © Francis G. Mayer/CORBIS

Anthony Annandono, 19, 28, 31, 55, 63(bottom), 97, 103

Dover Publications, Inc., 14 (top), 25, 51, 53, 54, 57, 58, 65, 69, 72, 76 (top), 77, 79, 80, 88, 90, 92, 95, 99, 101, 102, 104, 105, 108

© Hulton Archive by Getty Images, 27, 32, 33, 35, 41, 64

© Kelly/Mooney Photography/CORBIS, 74

Library of Congress, 9, 13, 14 (bottom), 23, 38, 39, 42, 48, 49, 59, 62, 82, 84

North Wind Pictures, Inc., 10, 21, 29, 43, 45, 63 (top), 67, 70, 76(bottom), 78, 89

★ About the Author ★

Nathan Aaseng is an award-winning author of more than 160 nonfiction and fiction books for young readers, on a wide variety of subjects. Aaseng, from Eau Claire, Wisconsin, was a 1999 recipient of the Wisconsin Library Association's Notable Wisconsin Author Award.